DATE DUE

			PRINTED IN U.S.A.

San Diego CUISINE

A Sampling of Restaurants & Their Recipes

Compiled and Edited by

GWENN M. JENSEN

Two Lane Press

Publication date January 1993

ISBN 1-878686-09-7

Printed in the United States of America

Cover design, hand lettering, and text ornaments: Calvert Guthrie
Editing and text design: Jane Doyle Guthrie
Food consultant: Judith Fertig

10   9   8   7   6   5   4   3   2   1   93   94   95   96   97

Two Lane Press, Inc.
4245 Walnut Street
Kansas City, MO 64111
(816) 531-3119

Dedicated lovingly to my husband, Mogens; my daughter, April; and my late mother, Loraine Harmer. Thank you for adding such sweetness to my life.

▥ Contents

⛩ Acknowledgments

Special appreciation must go first to publisher Karen Adler, who invited me to write *San Diego Cuisine*. Thanks also to Marilyn Lewis, a former classmate who introduced me to Two Lane Press. To editor and food consultant Judith Fertig, I appreciated your insightful observations and encouraging words. Thanks also to editor Jane Guthrie for all the hard work. I am grateful to the San Diego Historical Society for sharing information and photographs with me.

A great big cheer must go to the many restaurateurs who took time out after long hard hours of serving customers to share their recipes with me. You were most generous, and I couldn't have done it without you.

◪ Introduction

Southern California is youthful. It is joggers, cyclists, runners, walkers, dancers, surfers, scuba divers—all actively involved. Toddlers to nonagenarians live enthusiastically in San Diego's pulsating energy. Health and vitality are the heart. The new, the colorful, and the fun can be found in "America's Finest City."

San Diegans often profess to prefer restaurants that serve only the plainest, most healthy, low-fat, high fiber, simple food. However, there is a youthfully indulgent side to San Diegans' tastes. Hedonistic sauces appear beside judiciously broiled seafood. Rich desserts appease the desire for a touch of something sweet and slightly naughty. San Diego restaurateurs cater to those who eat for sustenance and to those who eat for the pure pleasure and aesthetic enjoyment of it.

The ethnic mix of San Diego County gives vitality and variety to our dining. Do you like Mexican food? How about Chinese? Or Italian? Anyone for a Cajun meal? How about good solid American comfort food? Would you like a genteel afternoon tea done up British style? Fun, isn't it?

The best of San Diego County cooks and chefs took me into their kitchens. They let me snoop in huge kettles. They answered batches of questions. They shared their closest kept culinary secrets with me. I am grateful.

Now it is my chance to pass the magic whisk to you. I hope that you will relish the wisdom of San Diego County chefs as you use and enjoy their recipes in your own home. Here's to your health!

Gwenn M. Jensen

Beginnings

⫸ Gentleman's Tossed Green Salad

3/4 cup buttermilk ranch salad
  dressing
1 head iceberg lettuce, cleaned
  and trimmed
2 cups spinach leaves, cleaned
  and trimmed
3 cups romaine lettuce leaves,
  cleaned and trimmed
1/4 cup grated cheddar cheese
2 tablespoons bacon bits
1/4 cup croutons

Refrigerate ranch dressing for at least 24 hours before using. Tear iceberg lettuce, spinach leaves, and romaine lettuce into bite-sized pieces. Place greens, grated cheese, bacon bits, and croutons in a very large salad bowl. Toss with dressing until greens are evenly coated. Serve individually on chilled plates with chilled forks.

A delicious beginning, this also may be served as a meal in itself.

Serves 10

GENTLEMAN'S CHOICE
1020 San Marcos Boulevard
San Marcos, California 92069
(619) 744-5215

⣿ Plain Good Salad with Pine Valley House Dressing

1 large bunch romaine lettuce, rinsed and patted dry
6 radishes, sliced
1 carrot, pared and sliced or shredded
4 green onions, sliced
2 tomatoes, cut into wedges

Tear lettuce leaves into bite-sized pieces. Toss in radish slices, carrots, green onions, and tomatoes. Serve with **Pine Valley House Dressing**.

Serves 4 to 6

Pine Valley House Dressing

3/4 cup olive oil
1/2 cup red wine vinegar
1/2 cup chili sauce
1/4 cup diced tomatoes
1/4 cup dill pickle relish
1 tablespoon water
2 teaspoons Worcestershire sauce
1 teaspoon seasoned salt
3/4 teaspoon salt
1/2 beef bouillon cube
1/2 teaspoon minced garlic
1/2 teaspoon minced shallot
1/2 teaspoon white pepper
1/4 teaspoon fresh lemon juice
2 hard-cooked eggs, finely chopped
Dash of cayenne pepper

Combine all ingredients, then refrigerate until needed.

Makes 2 cups

PINE VALLEY HOUSE RESTAURANT
Old Highway 80
Pine Valley, California 91962
(619) 473-8708

⫷ Cucumber Salad

1 European-style cucumber,
   10–12 inches long, or 2
   (6-inch) cucumbers
2 tablespoons chopped fresh
   dill or 1 teaspoon dried
1/2 cup white vinegar
1/2 cup sugar
1/4 cup water
1 teaspoon salt

Cut cucumber into paper-thin slices. In a medium bowl, layer sliced cucumbers, sprinkling dill between the layers. Set aside. Combine vinegar, sugar, water, and salt, and pour over cucumber mixture. Refrigerate for 4 to 5 hours before serving. (*Note:* May be prepared a day ahead.)

In Finland this is called "kurkkusalaatti."

Serves 4 to 6

DANSK RESTAURANT
8425 La Mesa Boulevard
La Mesa, California 91941
(619) 463-0640

◖ Broccoli Salad

4 cups broccoli florets
   (no stems)
1/4 cup plus 2 tablespoons
   crisply cooked bacon pieces
   (about 4 slices)
2 green onions, chopped
   (tops included)
3/4 cup raisins
1 cup mayonnaise
2 tablespoons cider vinegar
1/4 cup sugar

Combine broccoli, bacon pieces, green onions, and raisins in a large salad bowl. In a small bowl, whisk mayonnaise, vinegar, and sugar until well blended. Pour over ingredients in the salad bowl, stir, and chill before serving.

Serves 6

QUAIL'S INN
1035 La Bonita Drive
San Marcos, California 92069
(619) 744-2445

⦕ West Coast Vegetable Salad

1/2 onion, finely chopped
1 bell pepper, finely chopped
3 carrots, thinly sliced
3 stalks celery, sliced
1 (16-ounce) can French-style
    green beans, drained
1 (16-ounce) can white corn,
    drained
1 (16-ounce) can petite peas,
    drained
1 (4-ounce) can pimientos,
    chopped
1/4 cup chopped parsley
1/2 cup sugar
1/2 cup cider vinegar
1/4 cup red wine vinegar
2 tablespoons water
Salt and pepper to taste

Combine first 9 ingredients and set aside.

In a bowl, stir together sugar, vinegars, water, and seasonings. Pour over vegetables and chill before serving. (*Note:* Keeps well in the refrigerator.)

Serves 8

SQUARE ONE
119 North Main Street
Fallbrook, California 92028
(619) 728-5154

⟨ Ensalada Cobb in Concha Shells

1 head iceberg lettuce
1 bunch romaine lettuce
6 medium tomatoes, cubed
3 large avocados, peeled and
    cubed
6 strips cooked bacon,
    crumbled
2/3 cup crumbled blue cheese
2/3 cup cubed Monterey Jack
    cheese
2/3 cup cubed cheddar cheese
Herb salad dressing (any type)
6 orange slices, membrane
    removed

Wash lettuce, saving 6 attractive romaine leaves for garnish. Chop remaining greens into 2-inch pieces and toss lightly. Add tomatoes, avocado, bacon, and cheeses, and toss along with enough salad dressing to moisten lightly.

Place **Concha Shells** in 6 medium-sized individual salad bowls for base support. Arrange a single romaine leaf in each so that the leafy portion shows above the shell. Fill each shell halfway with salad, garnish with orange slices, and serve.

Serves 6

Concha Shells

6 large flour tortillas
Vegetable oil

Heat deep oil to 425 degrees in a large pot or deep fryer. Poke 10 holes in each tortilla. One at a time, place tortillas on top of hot oil. Position a large metal colander in the center of tortilla. Press down until tortilla is submerged in oil. Continue to fry, using colander to mold tortilla into a bowl shape. (*Note:* This will take about 30 seconds per tortilla.) Remove tortilla from oil and drain immediately. Allow to cool before filling with salad.

Makes 6

HAMBURGUESA
2754 Calhoun Street
San Diego, California 92110
(619) 295-0584

Warm Veal Sweetbread Salad with Honey-Mustard Dressing

1-1/2 pounds fresh veal
    sweetbreads
6 tablespoons peanut oil
Salt and pepper to taste
4 cups mixed salad greens
    (curly or Belgian endive,
    lolla biondo, green oak leaf
    lettuce, mâche, etc.), rinsed
    and patted dry
2 teaspoons champagne
    vinegar
1 shallot, chopped
1 bunch small radishes, sliced
1 bunch fresh chervil
4 edible flowers (pansies or
    nasturtiums)

Rinse sweetbreads with cold water. Remove thick skins and break sweetbreads into bite-sized pieces. Place on a kitchen towel to dry. Heat 4 tablespoons peanut oil in a large frying pan and place over high heat. Sauté sweetbreads until crisp. Season with salt and pepper, then remove from heat and keep warm.

Place salad greens in a large bowl and carefully mix with combined 2 tablespoons peanut oil, champagne vinegar, and shallot. Season with salt and pepper. To serve, place salad mixture on 4 large chilled salad plates, then arrange 5 to 6 pieces of sweetbreads and sliced radishes on top of each. Spoon on **Honey-Mustard Dressing** and decorate each plate with 4 to 5 chervil leaves and a flower.

Serves 4

Honey-Mustard Dressing

1/2 tablespoon Dijon mustard
1 tablespoon champagne
    vinegar
1 tablespoon honey
2 tablespoons peanut oil
Salt and cayenne pepper to
    taste

Combine mustard, vinegar, and honey, then slowly whisk in peanut oil. Season with cayenne pepper and salt.

Makes about 1/4 cup

MILLE FLEURS
6009 Paseo Delicias
Rancho Santa Fe, California 92067
(619) 756-3085

ⓘ Orange Sesame Chicken Salad

2 (6–8-ounce) boneless,
  skinless chicken breasts
1/2 cup soy sauce
1 tablespoon garlic powder
1/8 teaspoon allspice
2 tablespoons fresh orange
  juice
1/2 cup bottled sweet-and-sour
  sauce
3 tablespoons mayonnaise
1 teaspoon sesame oil
1 teaspoon rice wine vinegar
1 large head lettuce (any
  variety)
1 cup mandarin orange
  sections, canned or fresh
24 fresh pea pods, trimmed
Toasted sesame seeds

Marinate chicken breasts in soy sauce, garlic powder, and allspice for 1 hour. After marinating, broil breasts for about 10 minutes or until done. Mix together a dressing of orange juice, sweet-and-sour sauce, mayonnaise, oil, and vinegar. Arrange lettuce on individual plates, and garnish with orange wedges and fresh pea pods. Slice broiled chicken breasts and arrange on top of salad greens while still hot. Drizzle with orange dressing, sprinkle with toasted sesame seeds, and serve immediately.

Serves 4

BIG STONE LODGE
12237 Old Pomerado Road
Poway, California 92064
(619) 748-1135

⟨⟨ Marinated Grilled Chicken Salad

4 boneless, skinless chicken
  breast halves (about 1-1/4
  pounds total)
2 cups vegetable oil
1/2 cup soy sauce
1 tablespoon coarsely ground
  pepper
1-1/2 teaspoons fresh lemon
  juice
8 large green lettuce leaves
12 cups mixed chopped
  iceberg lettuce, shredded
  carrots, and shredded red
  cabbage
4 tomatoes, cut into wedges
1 large cucumber, scored and
  sliced
1 large carrot, thinly sliced
1 cup sliced fresh mushrooms
1/4 cup chopped green onions
1 cup salad dressing
  (your choice)

Marinate chicken for several hours in combined vegetable oil, soy sauce, pepper, and lemon juice. Remove breasts from marinade and grill until still moist (do not overcook or char).

Place 2 lettuce leaves on each of 4 large salad plates. Distribute salad mix evenly among plates to form a border around lettuce leaves. Slice grilled chicken into 1/4-by-3-inch strips and lay on top of lettuce. Place tomato wedges, cucumber slices, carrots, and mushrooms attractively around edges of plates. Sprinkle with chopped green onions and serve with dressing on the side.

Serves 4 generously

CARLOS MURPHY'S
Several locations
6680 Convoy Court (Corporate Office)
San Diego, California 92111
(619) 576-3840

⦀ Avocado and Shrimp Vinaigrette

1-1/2 pounds medium shrimp, cooked, shelled, and deveined
1-1/2 cups coarsely chopped tomatoes
1 green bell pepper, seeded and diced
1-1/2 cups thinly sliced celery
1 red onion, thinly sliced
1 cup bottled salsa
2 tablespoons avocado or olive oil
2 tablespoons fresh lemon or lime juice
Salt to taste (optional)
2 cups shredded lettuce
2 large ripe avocados, peeled and sliced
Lemon wedges
Cocktail sauce or dressing (optional)

In a bowl, lightly mix shrimp, tomatoes, green pepper, celery, and red onion. In another bowl, combine salsa, oil, lemon juice, and salt. Pour over shrimp mixture, then cover and refrigerate for 4 hours.

Divide shredded lettuce among 6 individual salad plates and spoon shrimp mixture over the top of each. Arrange avocado slices beside shrimp and garnish with lemon wedges. If desired, serve with cocktail sauce or dressing on the side.

Serves 6

BEV'S KOZY KITCHEN
138 West Grand Avenue
Escondido, California 92027
(619) 745-9265

⟨ Cream of Spinach and Sorrel Soup with Trout Quenelles

4 tablespoons butter
1/2 cup chopped white onion
4 cloves garlic, chopped
6 cups spinach leaves, rinsed
    and patted dry
2 tablespoons all-purpose flour
4 cups cold chicken stock
1 cup heavy cream
Salt and pepper to taste
1 bunch fresh sorrel, rinsed
    and julienned
Small amount of slightly
    whipped cream
Croutons

Melt butter in a soup pot over medium heat. Add onions and garlic and cook for 2 minutes. Stir in spinach. After spinach wilts, add flour and mix well. Add 1-1/3 cups cold chicken stock to mixture and bring to a boil. Stir in remaining stock and cream. Bring to a boil again, then season with salt and pepper. Transfer to a blender or food processor and mix. To serve, put 3 to 5 **Trout Quenelles** into each of 4 warm soup bowls along with soup and 2 tablespoons of sorrel strips. Garnish with slightly whipped cream and croutons.

Serves 4

Trout Quenelles

6 ounces fresh trout fillet
Salt and cayenne pepper to
    taste
1 egg white
1/2 cup heavy cream
1 cup dry white wine
2 cups water

Cut fish into bite-sized pieces. Season with salt and cayenne pepper, then place in the freezer for 15 minutes. Whirl trout pieces in a food processor for 10 seconds, then add egg white and cream, blending to a smooth mousse consistency. Refrigerate until mixture sets, then, using 2 teaspoons, form mixture into oval shapes. In a saucepan, combine water and wine, and bring to a simmer. Drop quenelles into the hot liquid and poach for about 3 minutes. (*Note:* Quenelles will float to the surface when cooked.)

Makes 12 to 15

MILLE FLEURS
6009 Paseo Delicias
Rancho Santa Fe, California 92067
(619) 756-3085

ⓚ Gazpacho

2 cucumbers, peeled, seeded,
  and chopped
1 onion, chopped
1 green bell pepper, chopped
1/4 cup chopped canned
  pimientos
1/3 cup chopped fresh cilantro
3 large tomatoes, seeded and
  chopped
2 cups tomato sauce
3 tablespoons red wine vinegar
3 tablespoons olive oil
1-1/2 tablespoons granulated
  garlic
1 cup chicken broth
Salt and pepper to taste
Chopped fresh basil and
  oregano to taste
Tabasco sauce to taste
Garlic croutons

Reserve half the cucumbers, onion, green pepper, pimientos, cilantro, and tomatoes. Transfer the other half to a food processor or blender and whirl with tomato sauce, vinegar, oil, garlic, broth, and seasonings until fairly smooth. Add reserved vegetables and chill. Serve cold, garnished with garlic croutons.

Serves 6

SQUARE ONE
119 North Main Street
Fallbrook, California 92028
(619) 728-5124

ᛚᚷ Chicken and Cheese Soup

1 (3–4-pound) whole chicken,
   cooked, boned, and diced
1-1/2 cups chicken stock
3 large carrots, peeled and
   sliced
3 stalks celery, minced
1/2 cup minced onion
1 (14-ounce) can cream of
   chicken soup
1 soup can water or milk
1 cup grated longhorn cheese

Simmer carrots, celery, and onion in chicken broth until tender, about 15 minutes. Add canned soup, milk or water, and reserved diced chicken, and heat through. Stir in grated cheese. Heat mixture until cheese melts (do not allow to boil), then serve.

Serves 8

SQUARE ONE
119 North Main Street
Fallbrook, California 92028
(619) 728-5154

⫷ Casa de Pico's Tortilla Soup

1 (3–4-pound) whole chicken
3 medium onions (1 peeled and
   left whole, 2 diced)
6–8 cups water
Salt to taste
1 clove garlic, minced
3 red bell peppers, diced
3 tablespoons chopped fresh
   basil
White pepper to taste
1 cup tomato sauce
1 cup vegetable oil
12 corn tortillas, cut into
   1/2-inch strips
1 avocado, peeled and diced
1 cup chopped fresh cilantro
Lemon wedges

Mission Inn
Riverside maybe
has some chpd
canned tomatos +
a few chiles

Place chicken in a large pot with peeled whole onion, water, and salt. Simmer for 1 hour or until chicken is cooked through. Remove chicken and reserve broth. Refrigerate both (separately) for several hours.

Skim off fat from chicken broth and set aside. Bring broth to a simmer. Sauté garlic, diced onions, and bell peppers in a small amount of reserved chicken fat. Drain off fat and transfer vegetable mixture to simmering broth, along with basil, white pepper, and tomato sauce.

Fry corn tortilla strips in vegetable oil until crisp, then drain and place in a large decorative bowl. Cut cooled chicken into bite-sized pieces. Arrange chicken chunks in bowl with tortilla strips, and add avocado and cilantro. Pour hot broth over all. Garnish with lemon wedges and serve at once.

This traditional tortilla soup is good with a green salad and a cold beer.

Serves 8

CASA DE PICO
2754 Calhoun Street
San Diego, California 92110
(619) 296-3276

⫷ Cafe Del Rey Moro Tortilla Soup

4 medium tomatoes, peeled
   and quartered
4 tablespoons chopped onion
2 cloves garlic, chopped
4 tablespoons chopped fresh
   cilantro
4 tablespoons chopped fresh
   oregano
1 cup tomato sauce
4 cups chicken broth
1 teaspoon salt (optional)
8 corn tortillas
1 cup vegetable oil
5 ounces grated Monterey Jack
   cheese
1 avocado, sliced

Combine tomatoes, onion, garlic, cilantro, oregano, and tomato sauce in a blender or food processor, and whirl until nearly smooth. Transfer mixture to a large saucepan, stir in chicken broth, and bring to a boil. Lower heat and simmer for 20 minutes. Add salt if needed.

Cut tortillas into 1/2-by-2-inch strips. Fry in oil until crisp and lightly brown, then drain. Arrange strips in soup bowls, add Monterey Jack cheese, and ladle soup over all. Garnish with avocado slices and serve.

This is a hearty yet quick-to-fix soup.

Serves 6

CAFE DEL REY MORO
1549 El Prado, Balboa Park
San Diego, California 92101
(619) 234-8511

⫷ Sopa del Mar

1/4 pound red snapper, cut into
   1-inch squares
1/4 pound medium shrimp,
   peeled and deveined
1/4 cup vegetable oil
2 stalks celery, chopped
1/2 large bell pepper, chopped
1/2 onion, chopped
2 tomatoes, chopped
10 ounces whole peeled
   tomatoes
3-1/2 cups water
2-1/2 tablespoons clam broth
2-1/2 tablespoons chicken
   bouillon base
1 tablespoon granulated garlic
1 tablespoon monosodium
   glutamate (optional)
1/2 tablespoon salt
1/2 tablespoon white pepper
2–3 bay leaves
1-1/2 tablespoons chopped
   fresh oregano

Refrigerate fish and shrimp while preparing soup base.

In a large pot, heat oil and sauté celery, bell pepper, and onion until onion is golden. Turn off heat and add both chopped tomatoes and whole tomatoes. Add water and bring ingredients to a slow boil. Add clam broth, chicken bouillon base, garlic, monosodium glutamate, salt, and white pepper. Let boil for 5 minutes. Add raw fish and shrimp, followed by bay leaves. Cover and simmer over medium heat for 30 minutes. Stir in fresh oregano, simmer briefly, and serve.

Serves 6

CASA DE BANDINI
2754 Calhoun Street
San Diego, California 92110
(619) 297-8211

◖ Chiles Rellenos

4 long green chilies (mild
    variety)
4 strips Monterey Jack cheese,
    3 in. by 1/2 in. by 1/2 in.
2 tablespoons all-purpose flour
4 eggs, separated
Vegetable oil

Roast chilies in a hot broiler or over an open flame until skin turns black and blistered. Roll hot chiles in a clean kitchen towel and allow blackened skin to loosen as they steam. Peel off skin and remove all or most of seeds. Slit chilies vertically along one side and insert a strip of cheese into each. Fold sides of chilies around cheese strips to enclose completely. Roll stuffed chilies in flour and allow to rest for a few minutes so that flour coating will adhere.

Beat egg whites until consistency of meringue. Beat yolks, then carefully fold into stiffly beaten whites. Pour mixture over floured chilies. Heat 1/2-inch oil in a skillet. Transfer chilies into hot oil, spooning egg mixture over and around them. Turn and cook on all sides. Serve very hot.

Serves 2 to 4

RUPERTO'S MEXICAN FOOD
1010 West El Norte Parkway
Escondido California 92026
(619) 743-9720

ꝏ Mexican Potato-Cheese Fritters

6 large potatoes, boiled,
  skinned, and lightly mashed
1 cup grated Monterey Jack
  cheese
2 eggs
1/2 teaspoon granulated garlic
  or 1 clove garlic, minced
1/2 teaspoon salt
1/4 cup all-purpose flour, or as
  needed
Vegetable oil
Sour cream
Guacamole
Salsa

Mix lightly mashed potatoes with cheese, eggs, garlic, and salt. Add a small amount of flour to mixture to make potatoes stick together. (*Note:* Amount of flour needed will depend on size and type of potatoes plus size of eggs used.) Form potato mixture into 10 thick patties.

Heat a large skillet and pour in a small amount of oil. Fry patties 2 or 3 at a time until golden brown on each side. Serve each with a scoop of sour cream and a big dollop of guacamole. Offer salsa alongside.

¡Buen provecho!

Serves 8 to 10

EL TECOLOTE
6110 Friars Road
San Diego, California 92108
(619) 295-2087

╠ Cauliflower Fritters with Serrano Chili Sauce

3 medium heads cauliflower,
    leaves removed
1 cup dry white wine
2 cups water
1-1/2 cups grated Monterey
    Jack cheese
1 cup all-purpose flour
4 eggs, lightly beaten
Vegetable oil
Salt to taste

In a large pot, combine wine and water, and boil whole cauliflowers until just tender (do not overcook). Cool cauliflower and separate each head into 6 large pieces. Push a little grated cheese into the branches of each piece, pressing cauliflower and cheese together to make them adhere. Dip each piece into flour, coating all sides, then dip into beaten eggs. (*Note:* Eggs should stick to flour coating, but if they slide off give each piece a little more flour.)

Heat vegetable oil in a large skillet and fry fritters until golden. Season with salt and serve with **Serrano Chili Sauce.**

Muy sabroso when served with refried beans and rice.

Serves 8

Serrano Chili Sauce

1/2 onion, cut into thick slices
4 cloves garlic
2 or more serrano chilies, to
    taste
3 large tomatoes, quartered
1 large sprig fresh cilantro
1/4 cup vegetable oil

Put onion slices, garlic, chilies, tomatoes, and cilantro into a blender or food processor and chop finely. Heat oil in a saucepan. Add finely chopped vegetables and cook. Foam will form at beginning of cooking and will gradually disappear. When foam subsides, sauce is ready. (*Note:* The longer the sauce cooks, the thicker it will be.)

Makes about 3 cups

EL TECOLOTE
6110 Friars Road
San Diego, California 92108
(619) 295-2087

◖ Pollo Fundido

6 (12-inch) flour tortillas
1/2 pound grated Monterey
  Jack and cheddar cheese
  blend
3–4 cups shredded cooked
  chicken
4 cups White Cheese Sauce
Vegetable oil
Cilantro sprigs

Preheat oven to 350 degrees. Fill each tortilla with 2 tablespoons grated cheese and about 1/2 cup shredded chicken. Fold tortillas burrito-style, completely concealing chicken, and secure with wooden toothpicks if necessary. Heat oil in a skillet to 325 degrees and deep-fry fundidos until golden brown. Transfer to a baking dish, top with **White Cheese Sauce**, and sprinkle with remaining grated cheese. Bake for 5 minutes, then garnish with cilantro and serve.

Serves 6

White Cheese Sauce

1/2 cup (1 stick) butter
1/2 cup all-purpose flour
4 cups hot milk
2 cups shredded Monterey
  Jack cheese
Salt and pepper to taste

Melt butter in a large saucepan and blend in flour. Slowly stir in hot milk and whisk until smooth. Cook for 3 minutes, then stir in cheese. Season to taste.

Makes 4 cups

CASA DE PICO
2754 Calhoun Street
San Diego, California 92110
(619) 296-3276

᚛ Sausage Rolls

1 (12-ounce) package frozen
   puff pastry
3/4 pound ground sausage

Preheat oven to 375 degrees. Roll puff pastry dough into a 4-by-24-inch rectangle. Place sausage meat on a floured surface and roll with flour-coated hands until 24 inches long and about 1 inch wide. Place meat roll in center of dough and bring one edge of dough over to cover sausage. Overlap opposite edge of dough to form a double layer of pastry on top. Turn roll over to position double layer on the bottom. Cut filled pastry into 4-inch lengths for a substantial appetizer, or 2-inch lengths for daintier treats. Transfer to a baking sheet with edges and bake for 30 minutes or until golden brown.

Serves 6 to 8

VINEYARD BAKERY
1115-1 East Valley Parkway
Escondido, California 92027
(619) 489-6458

⫷ Mozzarella in Carrozza

8 slices sandwich-style white or
  wheat bread
4 slices mozzarella cheese
4 eggs
4 tablespoons grated Parmesan
  cheese
1 tablespoon minced fresh
  parsley
Pinch of pepper
1/8 teaspoon salt
Bread crumbs
Vegetable oil

Sandwich each slice of mozzarella between 2 slices of bread. Beat eggs with Parmesan cheese, parsley, pepper, and salt. Dip each sandwich into egg mixture and coat with bread crumbs. Fry in hot, deep oil until golden brown. Slice into large triangles and serve.

Try these with marinara or Alfredo sauce as a variation.

Serves 4

LUIGI'S CUCINA ITALIANA
766 North Midway Drive
Escondido, California 92027
(619) 745-2250

℟ Guacamole

2 large ripe avocados
  (avoid overripe fruit)
1/4 cup finely minced onion
1/4 cup finely minced cilantro
1 small tomato, peeled, seeded,
  and chopped
Salt to taste
Few drops fresh lemon or lime
  juice
Warm tortilla chips

Separate avocado flesh from the skins by scooping it away with a large spoon. Mash avocados just enough to leave a few small chunks. Add onion, cilantro, and tomato, and season to taste. (*Note:* Mix all ingredients carefully so that guacamole does not turn into a paste.) Squeeze a few drops of lemon or lime juice into guacamole to enhance the color and keep it from darkening as quickly. Serve with large warm tortilla chips. Refrigerate unused portions in a tight container.

To help prevent avocado flesh from darkening, use wooden tools instead of metal ones.

Serves 4 to 6

EL TECOLOTE
6110 Friars Road
San Diego, California 92108
(619) 295-2087

⫸ Sake Shrimp with Tangerine Vinaigrette

12 jumbo shrimp, peeled and
    deveined
3/4 cup Spicy Sake Shrimp
    Baste
2 tablespoons julienned red
    bell pepper
2 tablespoons julienned yellow
    bell pepper
2 tablespoons julienned leeks
3 teaspoons julienned fresh
    ginger
4 (2-inch long) pieces
    cucumber skin, julienned
1/2 cup Tangerine Vinaigrette
6 orange slices, membrane
    removed
Cilantro sprigs

Cook shrimp on a hot grill while basting with **Spicy Sake Shrimp Baste**. Set aside.

Place vegetables in a strainer and cook in boiling water for 20 seconds. Evenly divide two-thirds of vegetables among 4 serving plates. Arrange reserved shrimp on vegetables, then top with remaining vegetables. Pour **Tangerine Vinaigrette** over all. Serve garnished with orange slices and cilantro.

Serves 4

Spicy Sake Shrimp Baste

1/4 cup garlic black bean paste
    (available at Asian markets)
8 cloves garlic
1/2 cup fresh ginger, minced
1/3 cup Vietnamese chili sauce
    (available at Asian markets)
1 cup honey
3/4 cup sake
1/2 cup sesame oil
1/2 cup vegetable oil
1/2 cup soy sauce

Place all ingredients in blender and whirl until smooth. Store unused portions in the refrigerator.

Makes about 4-1/3 cups

This is a wonderful oriental marinade that also complements chicken and other seafoods.

Tangerine Vinaigrette

1 cup fresh tangerine juice
1/4 cup rice wine vinegar
1 shallot, minced
2 cloves garlic, minced
1/4 cup mirin (sweet sake,
    available at Asian markets)
1 teaspoon mushroom soy
    sauce
2/3 cup vegetable oil
Salt and white pepper to taste

Whisk together tangerine juice, rice wine vinegar, shallot, garlic, mirin, and soy sauce. Add oil in a steady stream while continuing to whisk. Season with salt and white pepper. Refrigerate unused portions. (*Note:* May be made 2 to 3 days in advance.)

Makes about 2 cups

This delicious vinaigrette can be used on a variety of fresh salads.

CAFE JAPENGO
Hyatt Regency La Jolla
3777 La Jolla Village Drive
San Diego, California 92122
(619) 552-1234

⦃ Scampi

16 jumbo shrimp, peeled and
    deveined with tail intact
1/4 cup extra-virgin olive oil
4 teaspoons minced garlic
4 tablespoons chopped fresh
    parsley
4 tablespoons butter
4 cups whole fresh mushrooms
Juice of 4 lemons
4 cups dry white wine
2 cups Besciamella Sauce

Heat oil in a sauté pan. Sauté garlic and parsley briefly, then add shrimp and cook until color begins to change. Add butter, mushrooms, lemon juice, and wine. Simmer briefly. Stir in **Besciamella Sauce** and heat to serving temperature.

Serves 4

Serve with big wedges of Italian bread to get every last bit of the sauce. Excellent!

Besciamella Sauce

3 tablespoons butter
3 tablespoons all-purpose flour
2 cups hot milk
1/2 teaspoon salt
1/8 teaspoon white pepper

Melt butter in a medium saucepan and blend in flour. Allow mixture to foam together over low to moderate heat for about 2 minutes (do not allow to brown). Pour in about half the hot milk and whisk thoroughly. Simmer for 2 to 3 minutes, adding remaining milk plus salt and white pepper. When sauce becomes thick enough to coat a spoon, adjust seasonings and remove from heat.

Makes 2 cups

VALENTINO'S
11828 Rancho Bernardo Road
San Diego, California 92128
(619) 451-3200

⟪ Shrimp Filippi

24 large shrimp, peeled and
  deveined
1 cup olive oil
4 cloves garlic, minced
8 tablespoons (1 stick) butter
  or margarine
1 cup diced green onions
2 small tomatoes, chopped
1 cup sliced fresh mushrooms
4 tablespoons chopped fresh
  parsley
2 teaspoons dried oregano
1/2 cup Marsala wine
Salt and pepper to taste
Lemon wedges

Refrigerate cleaned shrimp while preparing sauce. In a sauté pan, sauté garlic in olive oil. Add butter and green onions, and cook for 2 minutes. Add tomatoes, mushrooms, parsley, oregano, and wine, and simmer for 3 minutes. Add shrimp to the sauce and simmer until shrimp turn pink. Season with salt and pepper and garnish each serving with a lemon wedge.

Serve this flavorful combination over cooked pasta.

Serves 4

FILIPPI'S PIZZA GROTTO
Several locations
9969 Mira Mesa Boulevard (General Office)
Suite 5
San Diego, California 92131
(619) 695-1441

◖ Sugar-Cured Salmon with Chinese Mustard

6 (8-ounce) king salmon fillets
3 tablespoons peanut oil

Lightly oil salmon fillets and coat with **Sugar/Spice Mix**. Grill over hot coals for about 4 minutes per side or until fish begins to flake. Serve with **Chinese Mustard**.

Serves 6

Sugar/Spice Mix

1 cup sugar
1-1/2 teaspoons dry mustard
1/2 teaspoon ground cinnamon
1 tablespoon cocoa powder
1 cup chili powder
1/4 cup ground cumin
2 tablespoons ground pepper
1/2 cup kosher salt

Combine all ingredients and use to coat seafood. Store unused portions in a tightly covered jar.

Makes about 2-3/4 cups

Chinese Mustard

1/2 cup dry mustard
1/2 cup sugar
Warm water

Combine mustard and sugar, and mix with enough warm water to achieve a creamy consistency. Refrigerate unused portions.

Makes about 1 cup

PACIFICA DEL MAR
Del Mar Plaza
1555 Camino Del Mar
Del Mar, California 92014
(619) 792-0476

⟪ Coho Salmon Carpaccio

3 (12-ounce) baby coho
  salmon, skinned and filleted
1 papaya, diced
3 passion fruit or guavas, diced
1 cup diced fresh pineapple
2 kiwis, diced
2 teaspoons grated fresh ginger
4 tablespoons apricot brandy
Juice of 3 limes
2 tablespoons sesame oil
Salt and pepper to taste
2 tablespoons grated Parmesan
  cheese
1 ounce fresh California
  truffle, julienned (optional;
  available at gourmet shops)

Flatten fillets lightly, wrap in plastic, and refrigerate.

In a large bowl, mix fruits with ginger and apricot brandy, and set aside for 30 minutes.

To serve, arrange fruit attractively on dinner plates and cover each portion with a raw salmon fillet. Sprinkle fish with lime juice, sesame oil, salt, pepper, Parmesan, and optional truffle. Serve at once.

Serves 6

U.S. GRANT HOTEL
326 Broadway
San Diego, California 92101
(619) 232-3121

◖ Ceviche

1 pound halibut or red snapper
   fillets
1/2 pound small shrimp, peeled
   and deveined
Juice of 2 limes
1-1/2 white onions, finely
   chopped
4 serrano chilies, chopped
3 large tomatoes, finely
   chopped
1-1/2 cups pimiento-stuffed
   green olives, finely chopped
3/4 cup fresh parsley, finely
   chopped
1 cup cilantro, finely chopped
   (reserve some for garnish)
1 tablespoon dried oregano,
   crushed
4 cups catsup
1-1/2 cups olive oil
1 (4-ounce) can chopped
   jalapeño peppers, undrained
1/4 cup Worcestershire sauce
Crackers or tortilla chips

Cut fish into 1-by-1/2-inch pieces. Put fish and shrimp into a bowl and squeeze lime juice over them. Marinate for 1 hour, then rinse and drain. Set aside.

While seafood is marinating, combine onions, chilies, tomatoes, olives, herbs, catsup, oil, jalapeños, and Worcestershire sauce. Pour sauce over reserved fish and shrimp and refrigerate overnight.

Serve garnished with chopped cilantro, accompanied by crackers or tortilla chips.

Serves 4 to 6

THE FIRESIDE
439 West Washington Avenue
Escondido, California 92025
(619) 745-1931

⫴ Scallops Parisienne

1-1/2 pounds medium scallops
4 tablespoons butter
2 cloves garlic, minced
4 shallots, finely diced
1 cup sliced fresh mushrooms
Salt and pepper to taste
1/3 cup brandy or cognac
2 cups heavy cream
Chopped fresh parsley

Heat butter in a large sauté pan. Add garlic, shallots, and mushrooms, and season with salt and pepper. Sauté for 2 minutes, then add scallops and sauté for an additional 2 minutes. Turn heat to high and add brandy or cognac. (*Note:* Chef Dave Pflieger cautions, "Stand back—it really flames." The overhead fan should be turned off to ensure safety.) Cook until brandy stops flaming, then add cream and cook for 2 or 3 minutes until sauce thickens. Garnish with freshly chopped parsley and serve.

Serves 4

THE FIRESIDE
439 West Washington Avenue
Escondido, California 92025
(619) 745-1931

◖ Coronne of Grilled Shrimp and Pink Grapefruit with Citrus Vinaigrette

20 jumbo white gulf shrimp, peeled and deveined
1-1/4 cups olive oil, divided
Salt and pepper to taste
1 whole pink grapefruit, peeled and sectioned
2 lemons, peeled, sectioned, and diced
1 orange, peeled, sectioned, and diced
3 cups fresh green lettuce, torn into bite-sized pieces
Snipped fresh chives

Toss shrimp with a small amount of olive oil. Grill over hot coals until done (about 2 or 3 minutes per side), then slice in half lengthwise. Season with salt and pepper and set aside.

Select the 4 best-looking sections of pink grapefruit and set aside. Dice remaining grapefruit sections and combine with diced lemon and orange sections. Mix fruit with olive oil and keep at room temperature.

To serve, toss lettuce with a small amount of olive oil and divide among 4 large salad plates. Alternate a piece of shrimp with a section of reserved grapefruit in a ring on each plate. Drizzle diced fruit mixture on the shrimp and grapefruit. Garnish with snipped chives and serve.

This tempts the eyes with its soft green and pink combination—a perfect choice for a bridal shower luncheon.

Serves 4

L'ESCALE
Le Meridien Hotel
2000 Second Street
Coronado, California 92118
(619) 435-3000

𝕴 Seafood Cannelloni

4 large manicotti shells, cooked
  al dente
1/2 pound halibut, sole,
  snapper, or sea bass, boned
  and cubed
1/4 pound sea scallops
1/4 pound bay shrimp, peeled
  and deveined
5 egg whites
1/3 cup heavy cream
1 teaspoon fresh lemon juice
1/2 teaspoon salt
Pinch of white pepper
Grated Parmesan cheese

Place cooked manicotti in a shallow pan of cool water, taking care not to tear shells. Refrigerate.

In a blender or food processor, puree fish, scallops, shrimp, and egg whites. Add cream, lemon juice, salt, and pepper. Continue to puree until mixture is thick and well blended. (*Note:* If any large pieces of fish remain, put mixture through a strainer to obtain a smooth texture.) Drain manicotti shells and, using a pastry bag or a spoon, fill each with seafood mixture. Steam stuffed shells in a double boiler for 15 minutes or until they are firm and spring back to the touch. To serve, slice and top with grated Parmesan.

These are also wonderful with white cheese sauce or red marinara sauce and a sprinkling of fresh Parmesan.

Serves 4

LAWRENCE WELK RESORT
8840 Lawrence Welk Drive
Escondido, California 92026
(619) 749-3253

Main Courses

Jansson's Temptation

3 tablespoons butter
2 large onions, sliced
4 medium potatoes, peeled and
 julienned
1 (3-ounce) can Swedish
 anchovy fillets (reserve
 brine)
1 cup half-and-half

Preheat oven to 400 degrees. Grease a shallow 2-quart baking dish and set aside. Melt 1 tablespoon butter in a large skillet and add onions, stirring occasionally. Sauté for 2 minutes or until soft but not brown.

In the prepared dish, alternate layers of potatoes, onions, and anchovies, beginning and ending with potatoes. Sprinkle with 1 tablespoon reserved brine. Dot with remaining 2 tablespoons butter and pour 1/2 cup half-and-half over the top. Cover and bake for 25 minutes. Remove cover and add remaining half-and-half. Bake uncovered for an additional 25 minutes. Serve hot or at room temperature.

This is an excellent light main course, frequently eaten in Sweden accompanied by dark bread or a large wheel of flatbread and a green salad.

Serves 6

DANSK RESTAURANT
8425 La Mesa Boulevard
La Mesa, California 91941
(619) 463-0640

⚓ Frijoles Refritos

1 (2-pound) package dried
  pinto beans
1/2 cup chopped onion
1/2 cup vegetable oil
Salt to taste

Soak beans overnight in a large quantity of water. Drain off liquid, transfer beans to a large pot, and cover with fresh water. Add chopped onion and bring to a boil. Lower heat and cook until beans are very tender, about 1 to 2 hours. (*Note:* A good test is to cook them until they're soft enough to mash on the roof of your mouth using only the tip of your tongue.)

Drain cooking water from the beans and reserve liquid. Heat oil in a large heavy saucepan and add beans a layer at a time, mashing each layer with a potato masher. Add cooking liquid back to mashed beans a little at a time. Watch carefully, as beans burn easily at this point. Add more water if needed. Add salt to taste and serve.

Enjoy frijoles refritos as a side dish with any Mexican food or as a vegetarian main dish with steamed flour or corn tortillas and salsa.

Serves 8 to 10

RUPERTO'S MEXICAN FOOD
1010 West El Norte Parkway
Escondido, California 92026
(619) 743-9720

Black Bean Chili

1 (2-pound) package dried
  black beans
10 cloves garlic, minced
3 stalks celery, finely diced
2 large carrots, finely diced
2 medium onions, diced
3-1/2 cups canned or fresh
  crushed tomatoes
1 (4-ounce) can chopped green
  chilies
3 bay leaves
2 tablespoons chili powder
1 tablespoon ground cumin
Salt and pepper to taste

Soak beans in water overnight. Drain off liquid and replace with enough fresh water to cover beans. Transfer to a large pot and simmer over medium heat.

Sauté vegetables and add to beans. Add remaining ingredients and cook until beans are very tender, about 45 to 60 minutes. Adjust seasonings and serve.

A marvelous vegetarian main dish that is especially good with hot cornbread.

Serves 10 generously

SQUARE ONE
119 North Main Street
Fallbrook, California 92028
(619) 728-5154

Fettuccine Matrigiana

1 pound fettuccine, cooked al
   dente
12 slices bacon, cut into small
   pieces
2 teaspoons minced fresh
   parsley
Pinch of pepper
1 cup dry white wine
3 cups marinara sauce or
   bottled meatless spaghetti
   sauce
1/2 cup grated Parmesan or
   Romano cheese

Sauté bacon pieces in a small pan. Add parsley and pepper while bacon is cooking. When bacon is crisp, add wine and cook for 5 minutes. Add marinara sauce and simmer for an additional 10 minutes. Add pasta and heat through. Sprinkle cheese over the top before serving.

Serves 6

LUIGI'S CUCINA ITALIANA
766 North Midway Drive
Escondido, California 92027
(619) 745-2250

✎ Linguine La Ver Nie

2 pounds fresh basil linguine,
   cooked al dente
1/3 cup olive oil
2 cloves garlic, crushed
2 shallots, sliced
2 large fresh tomatoes,
   chopped
California mild chilies, sliced
   (optional)
Pine nuts to taste
1 large bunch fresh basil,
   leaves only
Cracked pepper to taste
Freshly grated Parmesan or
   Romano cheese

While pasta is cooking, heat oil in a large sauté pan over high heat. Add garlic, shallots, tomatoes, chilies, pine nuts, basil leaves, and pepper. Toss a few times as the pasta cooks. Pasta and sauté should finish at the same time. Toss linguine with sautéed ingredients and serve in individual bowls topped with grated cheese.

Accompany with a fresh salad, a hot fresh bread, and a slightly chilled bottle of Sauvignon Blanc. To locate some of the many different types and flavors of fresh pastas available, look in the Yellow Pages under "pasta."

Serves 4

CAFE ELEVEN
1440 University Avenue
San Diego, California 92103
(619) 260-8023

Pasta Primavera in Marinara Sauce

1/3 cup diced carrots
1/3 cup diced mushrooms
1/3 cup diced zucchini
1/3 cup diced yellow squash
1/3 cup diced broccoli
1/3 cup diced black olives
1/2 cup extra-virgin olive oil
1 clove garlic, minced
2 cups marinara sauce
6 ounces angel hair pasta,
   uncooked
1/4 cup chopped fresh parsley
1/4 cup freshly grated
   Parmesan cheese

Steam carrots, mushrooms, zucchini, yellow squash, and broccoli until tender-crisp. Set aside. Heat olive oil in a large sauté pan. Briefly sauté garlic, black olives, and vegetables. Add marinara sauce and heat.

Cook angel hair pasta until al dente. Drain and keep warm.

Combine pasta and vegetables by gently folding together. Serve garnished with chopped parsley and Parmesan.

Serves 4

This flavorful combination offers an "intelligent" choice for the health-conscious aficionado of Italian cuisine.

VALENTINO'S
11828 Rancho Bernardo Road
San Diego, California 92128
(619) 451-3200

Joe's Linguine with Clam Sauce

1 pound linguine, cooked al
   dente
12 fresh little-neck clams,
   washed and cleaned, in the
   shell
1/2 cup olive oil
4 cloves garlic, thinly sliced,
   plus 2 tablespoons chopped
   garlic
1/2 cup water
1/2 teaspoon dried oregano
1/2 teaspoon salt
1/2 teaspoon pepper
Chopped fresh parsley

Heat olive oil in a saucepan. Add garlic and sauté until lightly browned. Add remaining ingredients except parsley and cook over medium heat until clams are heated throughout, about 15 minutes. Serve over cooked linguine, garnished with chopped fresh parsley.

Serves 4

This is an unusual dish with the clams served in the shell on top of the linguine. It makes an elegant appearance.

JOE'S ITALIAN DINNERS
403 West Grand Avenue
Escondido, California 92025
(619) 741-2935

⬭ Shrimp and Linguine Dijon

1 pound linguine, cooked al
    dente
1/2 cup (1 stick) butter
4 cloves garlic, minced
1-1/2 pounds medium shrimp,
    peeled and deveined
4 tablespoons Dijon mustard
2 eggs, lightly beaten
1-1/2 cups heavy cream
Chopped fresh parsley

Sauté garlic in butter. Add shrimp and cook until shrimp turn pink. Stir in Dijon mustard, eggs, and cream. Heat through and pour over cooked linguine. Garnish with parsley and serve.

Serves 4

LINO'S
2754 Calhoun Street
San Diego, California 92110
(619) 299-7124

◪ Camarones Calientes

1 pound linguine or fettuccine,
  cooked al dente
16 jumbo Gulf shrimp, peeled,
  deveined, and cooked
1 pound hot Italian sausage,
  cut into 1/2-inch pieces
2 tablespoons olive oil
1/2 green bell pepper,
  julienned
1/2 red bell pepper, julienned
1/2 yellow bell pepper,
  julienned
1 clove garlic, finely minced
1 tablespoon finely chopped
  jalapeño pepper
3/4 cup dry white wine
2 cups heavy cream
2 tablespoons butter
1/2 cup freshly grated
  Parmesan cheese
Freshly snipped parsley and
  cilantro

Brown sausage pieces in a skillet with olive oil. Drain on paper towels and wipe skillet clean. Over medium heat, sauté peppers, garlic, and jalapeño pepper in white wine for 2 minutes. Add shrimp and sausage, reduce heat, and simmer for 7 to 8 minutes. Pour off excess wine and add heavy cream to mixture. Cook over low heat until cream is heated through. Stir in butter, cover, and keep warm. (*Note:* Sauce may be prepared in advance and reheated.)

Distribute cooked pasta among 4 plates and scatter Parmesan cheese over the pasta. Arrange 4 shrimp on each plate. Spoon creamed sausage and peppers on top of pasta, taking care to evenly divide sausage chunks and various colors of peppers. Garnish with parsley and cilantro and serve.

Serves 4

SAN VICENTE INN AND GOLF CLUB
24157 San Vicente
Ramona, California 92065
(619) 789-8290

Grilled Shrimp Tacos with Tomatillo Mayonnaise

12 large shrimp, peeled and deveined
1/3 cup Carne Asada Marinade
4 (7-inch) flour tortillas
1 cup or more shredded green cabbage
1/2 cup Tomatillo Mayonnaise
2 tomatoes, diced
1 ounce grated Monterey Jack-cheddar cheese blend
2 teaspoons finely chopped cilantro
Sour cream (optional)

Marinate shrimp in **Carne Asada Marinade** for 1 hour. Drain marinade from shrimp and arrange them on bamboo skewers. Grill shrimp over hot coals and cook evenly, about 2 to 3 minutes per side (do not overcook).

Heat tortillas on a hot skillet and fill in the following order: shredded cabbage, **Tomatillo Mayonnaise**, grilled shrimp, diced tomatoes, grated cheese, chopped cilantro. Fasten tortilla together with a toothpick and serve promptly, garnished with sour cream if desired.

These are best directly off the grill. Serve with your favorite rice, refried beans, and fresh salsa.

Serves 4

Carne Asada Marinade

2 cups vegetable oil
1/2 cup soy sauce
1 tablespoon coarsely ground
   pepper
1-1/2 teaspoons fresh lemon
   juice

Combine all ingredients. Refrigerate unused portions in a tightly covered jar.

Makes about 2-1/2 cups

This marinade works well with beef, pork, and seafood.

Tomatillo Mayonnaise

1/4 cup tomatillo salsa
3/4 cup low-calorie mayonnaise
   or plain yogurt

Mix and refrigerate until ready to use.

Makes 1 cup

CARLOS MURPHY'S
Several locations
6680 Convoy Court (Corporate Office)
San Diego, California 92111
(619) 576-3840

❧ Shrimp and Scallops Robert Jarboe

1 pound large scallops
1-1/2 pounds large shrimp,
   peeled and deveined
4 tablespoons butter
2 shallots, sliced
2 cloves garlic, crushed
1/2 teaspoon fennel seeds
1/2 pound fresh mushrooms,
   sliced
4 canned artichoke hearts
Brandy
1 cup heavy cream
2 tablespoons chopped fresh
   parsley

Place butter, shallots, and garlic in a 10- to 12-inch sauté pan over high heat. Add scallops and cook until slightly brown and cooked halfway through, about 2 to 3 minutes. Add fennel seeds, mushrooms, artichoke hearts, and shrimp. Continue cooking until shrimp turn opaque, about 2 to 3 minutes. Add a small amount of brandy, ignite, and burn off alcohol, about 1 minute. (*Note:* Turn off overhead fan when you ignite alcohol.) Add enough cream to just cover bottom of pan. Stir in parsley. Continue cooking until shrimp are cooked and cream is reduced, about 3 to 4 minutes. Transfer shrimp and scallops to 4 small gratin dishes and serve.

Offer with rice or pasta and a nice crisp Chardonnay. Simple, elegant, and cooks in 10 minutes!

Serves 4

CAFE ELEVEN
1440 University Avenue
San Diego, California 92103
(619) 260-8023

✠ Sea Scallops on a Bed of Fava Beans

1-1/2 pounds sea scallops
2 tablespoons clarified butter
1 (750-ml.) bottle Cabernet
  Sauvignon wine
6 shallots, minced
1/2 cup (1 stick) butter
Salt and white pepper to taste
1/3 cup heavy cream, slightly
  whipped
2 tomatoes, peeled, seeded,
  and diced
Fresh chervil sprigs

Clean scallops, slice in half, and sauté in clarified butter for about 1 minute per side. Keep warm.

Put wine and shallots into a saucepan and simmer until liquid is reduced to approximately 2 tablespoons. (*Note:* Sauce will be deep purple.) While still on the stove, add butter 1 tablespoon at a time, whisking constantly. Season with salt and white pepper.

To serve, spoon a ring of **Fava Beans** in the centers of 4 dinner plates. Arrange scallops on top of beans, then spoon butter sauce around beans. Pipe or spoon slightly whipped cream around sauce. Garnish with diced tomatoes and a sprig of chervil.

Serves 4

Fava Beans

2 pounds fava beans, shells
  intact
1/3 cup butter
Salt and pepper to taste

Shuck beans and split in half. Blanch in boiling water for 1 minute, then drain and freshen in ice water. Sauté beans in butter until tender and season to taste.

Serves 4

MARIUS
Le Meridien Hotel
2000 Second Street
Coronado, California 92118
(619) 435-3000

⚜ Del Coronado Shore Plate

1 pound fresh fish fillets
Fresh dill
2 tablespoons capers
4 tablespoons Garlic Butter
1 pound bay scallops
12 large breaded and fried
   shrimp
8 breaded and fried calamari
   fingers
Lemon wedges
Green leaf lettuce
Parsley sprigs

Cut fish into 4 portions. Broil or grill and garnish each with fresh dill, 1/2 tablespoon capers, and 1/2 tablespoon **Garlic Butter**. Keep warm.

String bay scallops onto four 6-inch skewers. Baste each skewer with 1/2 tablespoon **Garlic Butter** and broil or grill. Keep warm.

To serve, arrange fish on 4 dinner plates, along with scallop brochettes, fried shrimp, and fried calamari. Garnish each plate with a large ruffle of green leaf lettuce, a lemon wedge, and a sprig of fresh parsley.

Accompany each portion with an individual cup of coleslaw and a generous serving of thinly cut fries.

Serves 4

Garlic Butter

2 cloves garlic
1/2 cup (1 stick) butter or
   margarine, softened
1/2 cup canola oil

Mince garlic in a food processor. Add softened butter and mix. Pour in oil in a steady stream while the processor is running. Pour into a clean covered jar and refrigerate.

Makes 1 cup

OCEAN TERRACE GRILLE
Hotel Del Coronado
1500 Orange Avenue
Coronado, California 92118
(619) 435-6611

⚓ Mustard-Crusted Salmon

8 (7-ounce) salmon fillets
2 cups white bread crumbs
1 cup dry white wine
4 tablespoons Pommery
  mustard
2 tablespoons chopped fresh
  basil
Salt and pepper to taste
2 tablespoons butter
2 cups chopped endive
2 tablespoons sugar
1/4 cup red wine vinegar
1/2 cup veal or chicken stock

Prepare crust by mixing bread crumbs, white wine, 4 tablespoons mustard, basil, and salt and pepper. Set aside.

Sauté endive in 2 tablespoons butter. Add sugar. Deglaze skillet with red wine vinegar. Add veal stock and cook until liquid is reduced and thick. Season with salt and pepper. Keep hot.

Preheat oven to 350 degrees. Pat crust mixture onto salmon fillets and bake fish for 12 minutes. Serve salmon on a bed of endive with **Mustard Sauce** around the outside. (*Note:* Crust mixture and endive may both be made up to 3 days ahead.)

Serves 8

Mustard Sauce

1/4 cup chopped shallots
1 cup dry vermouth
2 cups veal or chicken stock
1 cup heavy cream
2 tablespoons Dijon mustard
2 tablespoons Pommery
  mustard
2 tablespoons butter
Salt and pepper to taste

Cook shallots in vermouth until dry. Add veal stock and cook until reduced by half. Stir in heavy cream and reduce by half. Remove from heat and stir in Dijon mustard, Pommery mustard, and butter. Season with salt and pepper. Keep hot until serving.

EL BIZCOCHO
Rancho Bernardo Inn
17550 Bernardo Oaks Drive
San Diego, California 92128
(619) 487-1611

Barbequed Salmon Wrapped in Foil

4 (8-ounce) salmon fillets
2 tablespoons butter
1 carrot, diced
1 stalk celery, diced
5 fresh mushrooms, diced
4 tablespoons dry white wine
4 teaspoons chopped fresh
  rosemary

Grease 4 pieces of foil with a small amount of butter or margarine. Place a salmon fillet, skin-side down, on each. Distribute chopped vegetables evenly over fillets. Sprinkle each with 1 tablespoon white wine and 1 teaspoon rosemary. Tightly wrap each foil packet and grill for approximately 15 minutes over medium-hot coals.

Serve with fresh broccoli or other green vegetable for a colorful and delicious meal.

Serves 4

GENTLEMAN'S CHOICE
1020 San Marcos Boulevard
San Marcos, California 92069
(619) 744-5215

◾ Salmon Fillets in Shrimp Sauce

4 (6-ounce) salmon fillets
Juice of 1 lemon
2 tablespoons butter or
  margarine
1 medium onion, sliced
2 tablespoons chopped fresh
  parsley plus additional to
  garnish
1/4 cup dry white wine
Salt and white pepper to taste
Lemon slices

Sprinkle salmon with lemon juice and let stand for 10 minutes. Season to taste with salt and pepper. Heat butter or margarine in a large skillet, add fish, and brown for about 5 minutes on each side. Add onion and cook until golden. Stir in parsley, then pour in wine and simmer for 5 minutes. Transfer fish to a preheated platter to keep warm. Reserve pan drippings for **Shrimp Sauce**. To serve, pour **Shrimp Sauce** over salmon and garnish with lemon slices and fresh parsley.

Serves 4

Shrimp Sauce

2 tablespoons butter or
  margarine
1-1/2 tablespoons all-purpose
  flour
1 cup fish stock or a
  combination of 3/4 cup water
  and 1/4 cup dry white wine
  or diluted chicken stock
1 cup heavy cream
1/4 cup dry white wine
3/4 cup thinly sliced fresh
  mushrooms
1/4 pound bay shrimp, peeled
  and deveined
Salt and lemon juice to taste

Melt butter in a saucepan, then stir in flour. Pour in stock, cream, and reserved pan drippings from salmon. Add wine and simmer over low heat until mixture thickens. Add mushrooms and bay shrimp and simmer for 12 minutes. Season to taste with lemon juice and salt.

Makes about 2-1/2 cups

OCEAN TERRACE
Hotel Del Coronado
1500 Orange Avenue
Coronado, California 92118
(619) 435-6611

Salmon in Potato Crust with Special Tomato Sauce and Chives

4 (6-ounce) fresh salmon fillets
4 medium potatoes, peeled and
   finely julienned
4 cups vegetable oil
Salt and pepper to taste
3 eggs, beaten
1/2 cup freshly snipped chives

Preheat oven to 350 degrees. Heat oil in a large skillet to 375 degrees. Add half the potatoes and cook until golden brown. Remove from oil, drain on paper towels, and season with salt and pepper. Repeat with remaining potatoes. When all potatoes are cool, crush with hands between paper towels.

Dip salmon fillets in beaten egg and roll in crushed potatoes. Repeat until fish is thoroughly coated. (*Note:* Use all of potatoes and beaten eggs.) Bake coated fillets on an ungreased baking sheet for 15 to 18 minutes.

To serve, pool **Special Tomato Sauce** on 4 dinner plates. Put a salmon fillet on top of sauce and sprinkle all with freshly cut chives.

Serves 4

Special Tomato Sauce

3/4 cup (1-1/2 sticks) unsalted
   butter, softened
1 tablespoon minced shallot
1 tablespoon minced garlic
5 Roma tomatoes, peeled,
   seeded, and diced
1/2 cup dry vermouth
1/2 cup fish stock (optional)
Salt and pepper to taste

Sauté shallots and garlic in 1 tablespoon butter for 2 minutes. Add tomatoes and cook for 3 minutes over low heat. Add vermouth and fish stock and reduce liquid to half. Put tomato mixture and remainder of the butter into a blender or food processor and whirl until smooth. Add salt and pepper to taste.

Makes about 1-1/2 cups

BARCINO GRILL
Hyatt Regency La Jolla
3777 La Jolla Village Drive
San Diego, California 92122
(619) 552-1234

Mako Shark with Cilantro-Lime Butter

6 (8-ounce) mako shark steaks,
  3/4–1-inch thick
6 (1/4-inch) pats Cilantro-Lime
  Butter, chilled
2 whole tomatoes, chopped
1 bunch green onions, chopped

Preheat oven to 450 degrees. Fold 6 sheets of 12-by-16-inch parchment paper in half lengthwise and cut into heart shapes. Place one shark steak on right half of each heart and top each with a pat of **Cilantro-Lime Butter**. Scatter tomato and onions evenly over steaks. Fold left side of parchment pieces over steaks and roll edges, using small turns until each envelope is firmly closed all around to the tip of the heart shape (turn in point at end of fold to secure bag). Place bags on a well-oiled baking sheet and bake for about 15 minutes (paper should be well browned). Remove from oven, transfer each bag to a dinner plate, and serve immediately. Cut bags open with a sharp pointed knife.

Serves 6

Cilantro-Lime Butter

2 cups (4 sticks) butter,
  softened
1/2 bunch fresh cilantro,
  coarsely chopped
Juice of 1–2 limes

In a blender or food processor, puree cilantro with lime juice. Transfer to a mixing bowl and combine with softened butter. Divide mixture and roll into logs 1 inch in diameter. Wrap in waxed paper and chill or freeze. (*Note:* May be refrigerated for 2 weeks or frozen for 2 months.)

Makes about 2-1/2 cups

QUAIL'S INN
1035 La Bonita Drive
San Marcos, California 92069
(619) 744-2445

Grilled Swordfish on Wakame with Mango Lychee Relish and Lemongrass Essence

8 (7-ounce) portions center-cut
  swordfish
Pink peppercorns

Grill swordfish over hot coals until done, about 4 to 5 minutes per side. Place a strip of **Mango Lychee Relish** down the center of 8 dinner plates. Spoon **Wakame Seaweed** mixture down the sides of each strip of relish. Top each with grilled swordfish, pour **Lemongrass Essence** around the rest of the plate, and garnish with pink peppercorns.

Serves 8

Mango Lychee Relish

1/3 cup finely chopped fresh
  cilantro
2 mangoes, diced small
12 lychees, diced
1/8 teaspoon ground ginger
Juice of 1 lime

Combine all ingredients and store tightly covered in refrigerator.

Makes about 3/4 cup

Wakame Seaweed

1-1/2 ounces wakame (dried
    seaweed; available at Asian
    markets)
1 tablespoon sesame oil
1 tablespoon teriyaki sauce
1 tablespoon balsamic vinegar

Boil 2 quarts of lightly salted water and add dried seaweed. Cook for 1 to 2 minutes (do not overcook). Strain and season to taste.

Quickly sauté seaweed in sesame oil. Add teriyaki and balsamic vinegar. Adjust seasonings to taste. Keep warm.

Serves 8

Lemongrass Essence

2 tablespoons dry white wine
1 shallot, chopped
1 teaspoon finely chopped
    lemongrass
2/3 cup unsalted butter, cut
    into cubes

Pour wine into skillet. Add shallots and lemongrass, and reduce liquid by two-thirds. Add butter, a cube at a time, and mix well. Strain and season to taste.

Makes about 1/2 cup

U.S. GRANT HOTEL
326 Broadway
San Diego, California 92101
(619) 232-3121

⚜ Grilled Ahi with Orange-Pineapple Salsa

8 (8–10-ounce) ahi tuna steaks
Salt and pepper to taste
Cilantro sprigs

Grill tuna over hot coals until medium rare. Spoon some **Orange-Pineapple Salsa** on each dinner plate and top with a tuna steak. Before serving, garnish each with a ribbon of salsa and a cilantro sprig.

Complement these succulent steaks with green onion–flecked white rice.

Serves 8

Orange-Pineapple Salsa

2 shallots, minced
2 cloves garlic, minced
2 Valencia or navel oranges,
    peeled, seeded, and diced
1/2 red onion, finely chopped
1/2 jalapeño pepper, seeded
    and diced
1/2 fresh pineapple, cored,
    peeled, and sliced into 1-
    inch pieces
1/2 cup firmly packed brown
    sugar
1 cup rice wine
1/4 cup sherry
1 bunch fresh cilantro,
    chopped

Place all ingredients except cilantro in a large saucepan and simmer over medium-low heat for 20 minutes. Stir frequently. Just before serving, add cilantro and mix.

Makes 4 to 6 cups

ANTHONY'S FISH GROTTO
4120 La Jolla Village Drive
La Jolla, Ca 92037
(619) 457-5008

⚎ Mahi Mahi en Papillote

4 (8-ounce) mahi mahi fillets
1 cup diced fresh spinach
1 cup diced fresh tomatoes
4 teaspoons chopped cilantro
2 teaspoons capers
Juice of 2 lemons
1/2 teaspoon dried oregano
1/2 teaspoon dried basil
1/2 teaspoon dried thyme
1/2 teaspoon lemon pepper
4 tablespoons unsalted butter

Preheat oven to 350 degrees. Fold 4 pieces of 12-by-16-inch parchment paper in half lengthwise, then cut each into a heart shape. Open each sheet up and place 1 fillet on the right half of each. Divide the spinach, tomatoes, cilantro, capers, lemon juice, herbs, and lemon pepper evenly over the tops of fillets. Dot each with 1 tablespoon butter. Fold left side of parchment pieces over fillets and roll edges, using small turns until each envelope is firmly closed all around to the tip of the heart shape (turn in point at end of fold to secure bag). Put papillotes in a large shallow pan and bake for 12 minutes.

This specialty of Chef Nick Excell is like opening a gift-wrapped present at the table.

Serves 4

TORREY PINES INN
11480 North Torrey Pines Road
La Jolla, California 92037
(619) 453-4420

⟨⟩ Three Peppercorn Mahi Mahi with Warm Red Potato and Fennel Salad

4 (7–8-ounce) mahi mahi fillets
1 tablespoon pink peppercorns
1 tablespoon green
   peppercorns
1 tablespoon white
   peppercorns
1 tablespoon olive oil
1 bunch frisée or other lettuce
Roughly chopped fresh parsley

Preheat oven to 350 degrees. Crack peppercorns using the back of a pan and a cutting board. Heat a sauté pan and add olive oil. Press peppercorn mixture onto fillets and quickly sear in hot pan. Place in oven for 5 minutes to finish cooking.

To serve, divide lettuce among 4 large bowls. Spoon warm **Red Potato and Fennel Salad** into each bowl, and fill remaining space with **Tomato Coulis**. Place a mahi mahi fillet on top of each serving and garnish with roughly chopped parsley.

Serves 4

Red Potato and Fennel Salad

6 red potatoes, quartered
1 bulb fennel, julienned
1/3 cup chicken broth
1 red bell pepper
1 green bell pepper
1/2 red onion, julienned
1/4 cup niçoise olives
1/2 tablespoon minced garlic
2 tablespoons balsamic vinegar
1 tablespoon rice vinegar
1 teaspoon fresh lemon juice
1/2 teaspoon Dijon mustard
1 egg yolk or egg substitute
6 tablespoons walnut oil
2 tablespoons vegetable oil
Salt and pepper to taste

Cook potatoes in boiling salted water until al dente, then set aside to cool. Cook fennel in chicken broth until al dente, then let cool.

Roast peppers under the broiler. When cool, peel, seed, and julienne. Mix potatoes, fennel, peppers, onion, olives, and garlic.

In a small bowl, combine vinegars, lemon juice, Dijon mustard, and egg yolk, and whisk for about 30 seconds. Slowly add oil while continuing to whisk. Season with salt and pepper. Just before serving, combine vegetable and dressing mixtures and warm in a large sauté pan.

Serves 4

Tomato Coulis

1 tablespoon olive oil
2 shallots, coarsely chopped
6 Roma tomatoes, chopped
1/3 cup chicken broth
Salt and white pepper to taste

Sauté shallots in olive oil. Add tomatoes and chicken broth, and simmer for 15 minutes. Season with salt and white pepper, then transfer to a blender and puree until smooth. Strain and keep warm or cool down for later use.

Makes about 1-1/2 cups

BARCINO GRILL
Hyatt Regency La Jolla
3777 La Jolla Village Drive
San Diego, California 92122
(619) 552-1234

❧ Caribbean Sea Bass with Papaya Salsa

4 (8-ounce) sea bass fillets
4 tablespoons Jamaican Jerk
   marinade (available at
   gourmet or specialty
   markets)
2 tablespoons olive oil

Rub marinade on fillets and let stand for at least 1 hour.

Heat oil in a skillet and sear fillets until done, about 4 minutes per side. Place a heaping spoonful of **Papaya Salsa** on each fillet and serve hot.

Serves 4

Papaya Salsa

1 papaya, finely diced
1/4 cup diced onion
1/4 cup chopped fresh cilantro
1 serrano chili, diced
Juice of 2 limes

Combine all ingredients and refrigerate until ready to use.

Makes about 1-1/2 cups

TORREY PINES INN
11480 North Torrey Pines Road
La Jolla, California 92037
(619) 453-4420

Aldo's Fresh Trout Calamari

4 (8-ounce) whole boneless
    trout
Salt and pepper to taste
2 teaspoons Italian herbs
4 tablespoons all-purpose flour
2 cloves garlic, minced
1/2 cup (1 stick) butter,
    softened
1/2 cup olive oil
1 pound calamari, cut into
    rings
16 large fresh mushrooms,
    sliced
4 shallots, chopped
3/4 cup dry white wine
1/4 cup capers, drained
1 cup marinara sauce
4 tablespoons grated
    mozzarella cheese
4 tablespoons grated Romano
    or Parmesan cheese

Preheat oven to 400 degrees. Sprinkle whole trout with salt, pepper, and Italian herbs, and then coat with flour. Set aside.

Combine garlic, butter, and olive oil in a blender or food processor. Heat 4 tablespoons garlic butter in a sauté pan and sauté trout for 5 to 6 minutes. Put remainder of garlic butter into another sauté pan. Heat and quickly cook calamari along with mushrooms and shallots. Add capers and marinara sauce. Transfer trout to an attractive oven-proof dish, and top with calamari mixture and sprinkled cheeses. Bake until cheeses have melted, about 5 minutes.

Serves 4

This fast, elegant recipe may be doubled or tripled. Serve with pasta and a glass of Chablis or Chardonnay.

DANTE'S
9379 Mira Mesa Boulevard
San Diego, California 92126
(619) 693-3252

⚡ Wok-Charred Catfish with Red Pepper Fettuccine and Black Bean Sauce

6 (8-ounce) catfish fillets
3 tablespoons peanut oil
1-1/2 pounds fresh red bell
　　pepper fettuccine, cooked al
　　dente

Coat fish fillets with **Catfish Spice Mix**. Heat peanut oil in a wok. Cook fish on one side, turn, and fry until done (do not overcook).

Distribute freshly cooked pasta among 6 warm dinner plates. Arrange fish on pasta, top with **Black Bean Sauce**, and serve.

Serves 6

Catfish Spice Mix

2/3 cup sugar
1-1/2 teaspoons dry mustard
1/4 teaspoon ground cinnamon
1-1/2 teaspoons paprika
1 tablespoon cocoa
3/4 cup plus 2 tablespoons
　　chili powder
2 tablespoons ground cumin
1/4 cup ground pepper
1/4 cup salt
2 teaspoons ground dried
　　thyme
3 tablespoons ground dried
　　oregano
1 cup toasted sesame seeds

Combine all ingredients and store in a tightly covered jar.

Makes about 2 cups

Black Bean Sauce

1 tablespoon peanut oil
1/4 cup minced garlic
1/3 cup chopped scallions
1-1/2 teaspoons minced fresh
   ginger
1/3 cup seeded and diced red
   bell pepper
1/3 cup seeded and diced
   yellow bell pepper
3/4 cup teriyaki sauce
1 cup chicken stock
1/2 cup fermented black beans,
   rinsed and chopped
   (available at Asian markets)
1/4 stalk fresh lemongrass
1-1/2 tablespoons chili garlic
   paste (available at Asian
   markets)
2 tablespoons cornstarch
1 tablespoon sesame oil

Sauté garlic, scallions, ginger, and peppers in peanut oil. Add teriyaki sauce, 3/4 cup chicken stock, beans, lemongrass, and chili paste. Simmer for 10 minutes, then remove lemongrass. Mix cornstarch with remainder of chicken stock and stir into hot liquid to thicken. Stir in sesame oil and heat through.

Makes about 4 cups

PACIFICA DEL MAR
Del Mar Plaza
1555 Camino Del Mar
Del Mar, California 92014
(619) 792-0476

Margarita Chicken Kabobs with Lime-Herb Butter

1 pound boneless, skinless
  chicken breast, cut into
  1-inch cubes
1 cup fresh lime juice
4 teaspoons sugar
1/2 teaspoon salt
1 teaspoon ground coriander
1 clove garlic, minced
2 ears fresh corn, cut into 8
  pieces each
1 large green or red bell
  pepper, seeded and cut into
  1-inch chunks
Toasted pine nuts
Chopped fresh parsley

Place chicken cubes in a shallow pan. Combine lime juice, sugar, salt, coriander, and garlic. Pour over chicken and marinate for at least 30 minutes.

Thread chicken onto skewers, alternating with pieces of corn and pepper. Grill over hot coals for 15 minutes, basting with **Lime-Herb Butter** and turning frequently. Serve garnished with toasted pine nuts and fresh parsley.

Offer wild rice pilaf as a crunchy accompaniment to these flavorful brochettes.

Serves 4

Lime-Herb Butter

2 teaspoons fresh lime juice
1/8 teaspoon sugar
1 tablespoon minced fresh
  parsley
2 tablespoons butter, softened

Combine all ingredients and refrigerate until needed.

Makes about 1/4 cup

CAFE DEL REY MORO
1549 El Prado, Balboa Park
San Diego, California 92101
(619) 234-8511

Cajun Chicken Fricassee

1 large chicken, cut up
1/2 cup all-purpose flour
1 cup vegetable oil
2 large onions, chopped
Salt and pepper to taste
1 tablespoon chopped fresh
   parsley
1 tablespoon chopped green
   onion tops

Heat oil in a heavy pot. Dredge chicken pieces in flour and brown in oil. Remove chicken from pot and set aside. Brown onions in oil. Return chicken to pot and add water (about 1-1/2 quarts). Let simmer until chicken is tender, stirring occasionally to prevent meat from sticking. Liquid should become a thick gravy.

About 10 minutes before serving, adjust seasoning with salt and pepper add chopped parsley and green onion tops.

Enjoy this over pasta or rice.

Serves 4

CAJUN CONNECTION
740 Nordahl Road #114
San Marcos, California 92069
(619) 741-5680

Chicken and Sausage Jambalaya

1/2 pound smoked sausage,
    sliced into 1/2-inch pieces
1 pound boneless, skinless
    chicken breast, diced
1/2 cup chopped onions
1/2 cup chopped celery
1/2 cup chopped bell pepper
1 (8-ounce) can tomato sauce
1 (28-ounce) can tomatoes,
    cut up
3 cups uncooked rice
3 cups water
Salt and cayenne pepper
    to taste

Place sausage slices and chicken in a heavy pot over medium heat, stirring constantly to render fat and to brown. Season to taste and add onions, celery, and bell peppers. Sauté for about 5 minutes or until done. Add tomato sauce and tomatoes. Stir well and simmer for 15 minutes. Add rice, water, salt, and cayenne pepper. Cover and bring to a boil. Lower heat to simmer and cook until rice is done.

Serves 8

CAJUN CONNECTION
740 Nordahl Road #114
San Marcos, California 92069
(619) 741-5680

Chicken Fajitas

1 pound boneless, skinless
   chicken breast
1 teaspoon salt
1 tablespoon cracked pepper
1 tablespoon crushed fresh
   garlic
2 whole bay leaves
1 teaspoon paprika
3 tablespoons Worcestershire
   sauce
1 bunch cilantro, chopped
2 tablespoons vegetable oil
2 green bell peppers, seeded
   and sliced into strips
2 red bell peppers, seeded and
   sliced into strips
2 onions, sliced into strips
2 tomatoes, sliced into strips
Corn or flour tortillas
Guacamole
Salsa

Cut chicken breast into strips. In a bowl, combine salt, pepper, garlic, bay leaves, paprika, Worcestershire sauce, and cilantro. Stir in chicken strips and refrigerate, covered, overnight.

Heat oil in a skillet. Add chicken mixture and sauté for 2 minutes. Add peppers and onions and sauté until tender but not soft. Add tomatoes and cook for 30 to 60 seconds. Serve with warm tortillas, guacamole, and salsa.

Serves 4 to 6

HAMBURGUESA
2754 Calhoun Street
San Diego, California 92110
(619) 295-0584

San Vincente Curried Chicken

4 (8-ounce) boneless, skinless
   chicken breasts
1/2 cup chopped celery
1/2 cup chopped onion
1 clove garlic, minced
4 tablespoons butter
4 tablespoons all-purpose flour
Approximately 1 cup milk
2 tablespoons curry powder
Salt and pepper to taste
1 cup pineapple chunks
1/2 cup shredded coconut
1/2 cup white raisins
1/2 cup broken cashew nuts
1/2 cup chopped tomatoes
1/2 cup chopped green onion
1/2 cup pickled watermelon
   rind or chutney
4 cups cooked white rice
Mandarin orange slices
Fresh mint leaves

In a heavy pot, cover chicken breasts, celery, onion, and garlic with water and simmer until cooked, about 20 minutes. Strain broth and reserve. Remove chicken breasts, cool, and tear into bite-sized pieces. Set aside.

Melt butter in a saucepan. Stir in flour to make a thick paste. Add chicken broth slowly and stir to a thick sauce. Add sufficient milk to thin sauce to a gravy consistency. Simmer for a few minutes, then add curry powder, salt, and pepper. Fold in chicken pieces. Heat to serving temperature and keep warm. (*Note:* Curry may be prepared up to 24 hours in advance. Refrigerate and reheat. Cook rice just before serving.)

Place a large serving of rice on 6 to 8 dinner plates. Ladle curried chicken onto the rice and embellish each serving with some of each condiment. Garnish with mandarin orange segments and mint leaves.

This exotic-looking dish is delightful served with white wine or champagne.

Serves 6 to 8

SAN VICENTE INN AND GOLF CLUB
24157 San Vicente
Ramona, California 92065
(619) 789-8290

Healthy Enchiladas Suizas

1 (2-1/2 to 3 pound) chicken
3 cups water
1 onion, quartered
3 cloves garlic, bruised
Salt and pepper to taste
12 corn tortillas
3 cups Verde Sauce
1-1/2 cups canned chopped
   green chilies
1 cup grated Monterey Jack
   cheese
1/4 cup chopped black olives
3 cups finely shredded lettuce
2 tomatoes, chopped
6 green onions, chopped

In a heavy pot, simmer chicken in water with onion and garlic for 45 minutes. Drain, let cool, and shred. Season to taste.

Preheat oven to 350 degrees. One at a time, dip both sides of tortillas in warm **Verde Sauce**, fill with 2 tablespoons seasoned chicken mixture and 2 tablespoons chilies, roll into enchilada shape, and place on bottom of a 9-by-13-inch baking dish. Pour remaining **Verde Sauce** over enchiladas and sprinkle them with cheese. Bake for 20 minutes. To serve, sprinkle enchiladas with chopped black olives and garnish with shredded lettuce, chopped tomatoes, and green onions.

Serves 6

Verde Sauce

4 pounds fresh tomatillos
1 cup water
7 yellow chilies (optional)
1 onion, chopped
1 cup chopped cilantro
1/2 teaspoon salt
1/2 teaspoon sugar
1 teaspoon minced garlic

Boil tomatillos in water for 20 minutes. Drain and reserve cooking water. Cool tomatillos in cold water, then peel off outer brown skin. Transfer peeled tomatillos to a blender or food processor, add chilies, onion, cilantro, salt, sugar, and garlic in a food processor, and whirl until smooth, thinning with reserved water if necessary.

Makes about 4 cups

HAMBURGUESA
2754 Calhoun Street
San Diego, California 92110
(619) 295-0584

Pollo Cacciatore

4 chicken breast halves
1 cup dry white wine
1 pound fresh mushrooms
1/4 cup chopped bell pepper
1 cup sliced onion
1 cup minced celery
2 cups tomato sauce

In a small amount of water, precook chicken breasts until over half done. Wash and trim mushrooms, leaving whole.

In a saucepan, heat wine with mushrooms, bell pepper, onion, and celery. Add tomato sauce, followed by partially cooked chicken. Sauté for an additional 5 minutes or until chicken is cooked through.

Serves 4

LINO'S
2754 Calhoun Street
San Diego, California 92110
(619) 299-7124

♞ Maui Macadamia Nut Chicken with Pineapple Relish

4 boneless, skinless chicken
    breast halves
1/2 cup crushed macadamia
    nuts
1/3 cup finely chopped bread
    crumbs
2/3 cup all-purpose flour
4 eggs, slightly beaten
Salt to taste
4 tablespoons butter
Shredded fresh coconut

Trim any fat from chicken breasts and flatten slightly by pounding.

Combine macadamia nuts and bread crumbs and place on a large dinner plate. Pour flour onto another plate. Place eggs in a third shallow container.

Sprinkle chicken breasts lightly with salt. Press flour onto each breast until covered, then coat each with beaten eggs. Last, press macadamia nut–bread crumb mixture onto each piece.

Sauté coated chicken breasts in 2 tablespoons butter until cooked through and nut coating is golden brown. Remove chicken, add remaining 2 tablespoons butter to sauté pan, and cook until brown. Pour a small amount of browned butter over each chicken breast.

Serve with a dollop of **Pineapple Relish** and a sprinkling of shredded coconut.

Serves 4

Pineapple Relish

3/4 cup crushed or finely
    chopped fresh pineapple
    (or substitute canned)
2 tablespoons toasted shredded
    coconut
1/4 cup honey
1/4 cup mango or papaya puree
    (available at gourmet or
    specialty markets)

Mix all ingredients thoroughly and refrigerate unused portions.

Makes about 1-1/3 cups

LAWRENCE WELK RESORT
8840 Lawrence Welk Drive
Escondido, California 92026
(619) 749-3253

Chicken St. Tropez

4 (6-ounce) boneless, skinless
  chicken breast halves
1/4 cup all-purpose flour
1/4 cup olive oil
1/4 cup chopped garlic
1 cup fresh spinach, julienned
1/4 cup sun-dried tomatoes
1/4 cup chopped fresh cilantro
2 cups champagne or dry white
  wine
Salt and pepper to taste

Dredge chicken breasts in flour. In a sauté pan, lightly brown each piece on one side in olive oil. Turn chicken over and add garlic, spinach, sun-dried tomatoes, cilantro, and white wine. Cook for 5 to 7 minutes. Remove chicken from the pan and keep warm. Simmer pan juices to reduce until slightly thickened and serve alongside breasts.

This is an entree with spirited flavor and not too many calories.

Serves 4

TORREY PINES INN
11480 North Torrey Pines Road
La Jolla, California 92037
(619) 453-4420

Kung Pao Chicken

1 pound boneless, skinless
chicken breasts, cut into 1-
inch cubes
2 tablespoons cornstarch
3 tablespoons soy sauce
Vegetable oil
1/2 cup peanuts
1 tablespoon dried red hot
pepper, seeded and cut into
strips
1 teaspoon chopped fresh
ginger
1 tablespoon dry white wine
1 tablespoon sugar
1 tablespoon water
1 teaspoon sesame oil

Mix chicken cubes with 1-1/2 tablespoons cornstarch and 2 teaspoons soy sauce. Let stand for 30 minutes.

Stir-fry peanuts in small amount of oil, then remove and let cool. Fry chicken in oil and remove when done. Drain all but 2 tablespoons of oil from wok or frying pan and fry red pepper strips until they turn dark. Add ginger, wine, sugar, and remaining soy sauce. Mix remaining cornstarch with water. Add to hot sauce and stir until thickened and translucent. Stir in sesame oil. Add chicken cubes to sauce and heat until to serving temperature. Sprinkle peanuts over dish and serve.

Serves 4

CHINA WHARF
1020 West San Marcos Boulevard
San Marcos, California 92069
(619) 744-8888

Caneton à la Normande au Poivre Vert with Golden Apple Slices

3 (4-pound) Long Island ducks
Salt to taste
1/2 cup crushed green
   peppercorns or to taste
1-1/2 cups sugar
1-1/2 cups red wine vinegar
4 cups duck stock (or
   substitute veal or chicken
   stock)
1/3 cup Calvados brandy

In a heavy pot, cover duck necks and trimmings with water and simmer to make stock. (*Note:* Can omit this step if necessary and substitute veal or chicken stock.)

Season ducks with salt and crushed green peppercorns. Roast for about 1 hour at 375 degrees. When done, remove ducks from oven and keep warm. Pour off grease from roasting pan. Add sugar, vinegar, and duck stock. Simmer mixture over medium heat to reduce by half. Sauce should look like a light caramel syrup. Lower heat and add Calvados.

Remove breasts, legs, and thighs from carcass. Bone ducks, if desired, and place in the center of a large platter, surrounded with **Golden Apple Slices**. Reheat in oven, pour sauce over duck, and garnish with additional whole peppercorns.

Serves 6

Golden Apple Slices

6 apples
2 tablespoons sugar
1/4 cup white wine

Peel and core apples, slice very thin, and set in a buttered baking dish. Sprinkle with sugar and white wine. Bake at 375 degrees for 15 minutes or until lightly golden brown.

Serves 6

EL BIZCOCHO
Rancho Bernardo Inn
17550 Bernardo Oaks Drive
San Diego, California 92128
(619) 487-1611

Grilled Spring Lamb Chops with Garlic and Rosemary Butter Sauce

8 (4-ounce) lamb chops
Olive oil
Salt and pepper to taste
1/2 pound fresh green beans, trimmed
1/2 pound baby carrots, stems removed
1/2 pound new potatoes, peeled
1/2 pound baby turnips
2 tablespoons unsalted butter
Chopped fresh Italian parsley

Brush lamb chops with olive oil and season with freshly ground pepper and salt. Set aside.

Blanch green beans in boiling salted water, then place in ice water. Cut carrots and potatoes into oval shapes before cooking. Steam carrots until al dente; steam new potatoes until done. Boil and peel turnips. Set all aside.

Grill lamb chops on both sides for about 4 minutes or until medium rare. Melt butter in a large casserole and add vegetables. Season with salt and sprinkle with chopped parsley. When vegetables are warm and coated with butter, arrange on large warm dinner plates. Place lamb chops in the center of plates, gently spoon **Garlic and Rosemary Butter Sauce** over them, and serve warm.

Serves 4

Garlic and Rosemary Butter Sauce

Juice of 1 lemon
2 cloves garlic, minced
6 tablespoons unsalted butter, chilled
2 tablespoons roughly chopped fresh rosemary
Salt and cayenne pepper to taste

Bring lemon juice and garlic to a boil in a very small saucepan. Boil until almost dry. Whisk in cool butter, add chopped rosemary, and season.

Makes about 1/2 cup

MILLE FLEURS
6609 Paseo Delicias
Rancho Santa Fe, California 92067
(619) 756-3085

🦃 Veal Scaloppine alla Marsala

1 pound veal cutlets, sliced 1/4-inch thick
1/2 cup all-purpose flour
1/2 teaspoon salt
1/8 teaspoon pepper
1/4 cup (1/2 stick) butter
1/3 cup Marsala wine
1/4 cup chicken broth
1/2 pound fresh mushrooms, sliced
1 lemon, thinly sliced

Put veal cutlets on a large cutting board and pound each to a 1/8-inch thickness. Mix flour, salt, and pepper and use to coat veal pieces.

Heat butter in a heavy skillet but do not allow to brown. Quickly put in the cutlets, 1 or 2 at a time. Brown for 2 to 3 minutes on each side. Remove cutlets from pan as they finish and set aside. After browning all cutlets, return them to skillet and pour Marsala over all. Cook for an additional 8 minutes, then transfer to a warm serving platter.

Add chicken broth and mushrooms to pan drippings, stir until blended, and simmer until gravy begins to thicken. Pour gravy over cutlets and serve garnished with lemon slices.

Serves 4 to 6

JOE'S ITALIAN DINNERS
403 West Grand Avenue
Escondido, California 92025
(619) 741-2935

❧ Piccata alla Marsala with Tricolor Linguine

1-1/2 pounds veal tenderloin,
   cut into 2-ounce medallions
About 1/4 cup (1/2 stick) butter
Salt and pepper to taste
1 zucchini, sliced diagonally
12 baby carrots, peeled
3 cups tricolor linguine,
   cooked al dente and kept hot

Sauté veal medallions in small amount of butter and season with salt and pepper. Blanch carrots in boiling water, then quickly cool in cold water. Prepare zucchini slices in the same manner. Toss hot, freshly boiled pasta with some of the butter and toss the vegetables, separately, with the remainder. To serve, pour **Marsala Sauce** on 4 dinner plates to cover, then make a nest of pasta in the center of each. Place 3 veal medallions around the pasta, and garnish each medallion with a carrot between 2 pieces of zucchini.

This colorful, festive presentation is worthy of a grand occasion!

Serves 4

Marsala Sauce

1 tablespoon butter
5 shallots, chopped
2 or 3 black peppercorns
2 bay leaves
1/2 teaspoon thyme
1 cup Marsala wine
2 cups veal or chicken stock

Sauté shallots and seasonings in butter, then deglaze pan with Marsala. Simmer and reduce mixture to one-fourth. Add veal stock and reduce again to desired thickness. Season to taste. Strain off herbs and discard.

Makes about 1-1/2 cups

L'ESCALE
Le Meridien Hotel
2000 Second Street
Coronado, California 92118
(619) 435-3000

✶ Milanesa con Papas

2 pounds top-quality round
   steak, sliced 1/8-inch thick
1 cup plain dry bread crumbs
1/2 teaspoon salt
1/4 teaspoon pepper
1/4 teaspoon granulated garlic
1 bay leaf (optional)
2 eggs, lightly beaten
Vegetable oil
Guacamole

Pound meat over a hard surface with a flat instrument. (*Note:* Do not use a regular kitchen meat pounder; it can make holes in the thin slices of meat. A flat piece of wood, the bottom of a heavy pot, or even a rolling pin will work.) Cut into serving pieces and set aside.

Put bread crumbs, salt, pepper, garlic, and bay leaf in a blender or food processor and pulverize. Dip pieces of steak into beaten egg, then pat crumb mixture onto each, pressing firmly. Heat a large skillet, add enough oil to coat the bottom, and rapidly fry steak pieces on both sides (do not overcook or allow either coating or steaks to burn). Serve with **Mexican Fried Potatoes** and a garnish of guacamole.

Serves 4

Mexican Fried Potatoes

4 large potatoes, cooked,
   peeled, and thickly sliced
Granulated garlic or garlic salt
Vegetable oil

After removing steak from the pan, add a little more oil if needed. Season potato slices with granulated garlic or garlic salt and fry until golden.

Serves 4

EL TECOLOTE
6110 Friars Road
San Diego, California 92108
(619) 295-2087

Corned Beef and Cabbage

1 pound corned beef, cubed or
  sliced
2 heads green cabbage, halved
4 potatoes, cubed
2 onions, sliced
4 carrots, peeled and sliced
4 tablespoons pickling spice
1/4 pound (1/2 stick) butter
1 teaspoon garlic powder
1 cup water
Fresh parsley sprigs

Place all ingredients in a large heavy pot, cover, and simmer for 45 minutes to 60 minutes. Arrange on a large serving plate and garnish with fresh parsley.

Serve this hearty traditional favorite with rye bread and butter.

Serves 4

McDINI'S
105 East Eighth Street
National City, California 91950
(619) 474-6771

⚜ Longhorn Italian-Style Burgers

1 pound very lean ground beef
Salt and pepper to taste
8 thick slices sourdough bread
4 tablespoons butter or
    margarine
Garlic salt to taste
1 cup shredded mozzarella
    cheese
4 slices provolone cheese
4 slices red onion
4 slices tomato
1-1/3 cups marinara sauce
    (optional)
4 large lettuce leaves

Mix ground beef with salt and pepper and form into 4 large patties. Grill until done to taste and keep warm.

Spread both sides of bread slices with butter or margarine and brown both sides on a griddle or large skillet. Place each hamburger patty on a slice of grilled bread, sprinkle with garlic salt, top with a slice of provolone, and sprinkle with grated mozzarella. (*Note:* Cheese should melt from heat of burger; if it needs help, put into a warm, not hot, oven.) Serve other slice of bread on the side. Decorate plates with lettuce and slices of tomato and onion. If marinara sauce is desired, heat it up and serve on the side.

Serves 4

LONGHORN CAFE
6519 Mission Gorge Road
San Diego, California 92120
(619) 283-0831

Swiss Steak

2 pounds eye of round steak
1/2 clove garlic
3 tablespoons all-purpose flour
1/2 teaspoon meat tenderizer
Celery salt to taste
1/4 cup sesame oil
1/2 cup chopped white onion
1 cup chopped carrots
1/2 cup chopped celery
1 cup tomato sauce
1/3 cup Burgundy wine

Preheat oven to 300 degrees. Rub meat with garlic, then coat both sides with flour, tenderizer, and celery salt. Pound coating into steak with a meat mallet or the edge of a sturdy saucer. Dust off excess flour coating and brown meat in sesame oil. Transfer to a large baking dish, and add onions, carrots, and celery. Mix tomato sauce with Burgundy wine and pour over all. Cover and bake for 2 hours. Serve warm.

Bev makes gravy from the pan drippings and serves it with real, made-from-scratch mashed potatoes.

Serves 4

BEV'S KOZY KITCHEN
138 West Grand Avenue
Escondido, California 92027
(619) 745-9265

Steak Fromage

4 (6-ounce) filets mignons
8 ounces blue cheese
4 slices bacon
1/2 cup (1 stick) butter
1/2 cup dry white wine
4 cloves garlic, minced
4 shallots, minced
2 cups sliced fresh mushrooms
4 tablespoons chopped fresh
    parsley
Salt and pepper to taste

Cut a slit in the side of each steak and stuff with blue cheese. Wrap a slice of bacon around each fillet and secure with a toothpick.

Combine butter, wine, garlic, shallots, mushrooms, and parsley in a sauté pan. Sauté over medium heat for 3 or 4 minutes until mushrooms are tender. Set aside.

Broil steaks to desired degree of doneness and serve smothered in mushroom sauce.

Serves 4

THE FIRESIDE
439 West Washington Avenue
Escondido, California 92025
(619) 745-1931

Carne Asada Tacos

1 pound carne asada, sliced
  and marinated
2 tablespoons vegetable oil
Salt and pepper to taste
8 corn tortillas
1/2 cup diced tomatoes
1 avocado, peeled and diced
1/3 cup diced onion
1/2 bunch fresh cilantro,
  minced
Salsa (optional)

Heat a griddle or skillet until very hot. Add oil and quickly cook carne asada, turning and seasoning with salt and pepper. Remove meat from griddle and keep warm.

Steam tortillas or warm them on hot griddle. Overlap 2 tortillas for each taco to create double thickness in the middle. Fill hot tortillas with meat, tomatoes, avocado, onion, and cilantro. Serve with your favorite salsa and lots of napkins!

Serves 4

RUPERTO'S MEXICAN FOOD
1010 West El Norte Parkway
Escondido, California 92026
(619) 743-9720

◪ Especial de la Casa de Bandini

2 pounds top sirloin, sliced into
    strips
1 cup beer
Juice of 1 lime
1/2 teaspoon minced garlic
2 drops Tabasco sauce
1/4 teaspoon dried marjoram
1/2 teaspoon salt or to taste
Corn tortillas
Guacamole
Salsa

Combine beer, lime juice, garlic, Tabasco, marjoram, and salt, and use to marinate sirloin strips overnight.

Grill strips until tender and serve with hot corn tortillas, guacamole, and salsa.

Serves 6

CASA DE BANDINI
2754 Calhoun Street
San Diego, California 92110
(619) 297-8211

Tournedos of Beef with Blue Crab and Pepper Vodka

4 (2-1/2 to 3-ounce) beef
   tenderloin steaks; narrow
   cut, cleaned but not
   pounded
2 (3/4-inch thick) slices
   Hawaiian bread
8 teaspoons butter
2 teaspoons chopped garlic
4 slices Roma tomato
2 tablespoons freshly grated
   Romano cheese
Salt and freshly ground pepper
   to taste
3 ounces (scant 1/2 cup)
   pepper vodka
2 teaspoons chopped shallot
1/4 cup beef broth
2 tablespoons heavy cream
4 ounces blue crab meat,
   cooked

Prepare 4 large croutons from Hawaiian bread, using a round cutter the same diameter as the meat. Spread each crouton with 1 teaspoon butter and toast very lightly in the oven. Top each piece with 1/2 teaspoon chopped garlic, a slice of tomato, and 1/2 tablespoon grated Romano cheese, then bake until crisp.

Heat a small sauté pan. Season meat with salt and pepper, and quickly sear on both sides in remaining butter. Add half the vodka and flame. Remove meat from pan, sauté shallot, and pour in beef broth and cream. Simmer and reduce to thicken. Adjust seasonings and finish with remaining vodka. Stir in crabmeat.

To serve, place a crouton on each of 4 dinner plates, top each with a steak, and spoon on crabmeat sauce.

Serves 4

PRINCE OF WALES
Hotel Del Coronado
1500 Orange Avenue
Coronado, California 92118
(619) 435-6611

Buffalo Tenderloin with Cranberries

2-1/2 pounds buffalo (or beef) tenderloin, untrimmed (available at the Farmer's Market or from Exo, a wholesaler)
Salt and pepper to taste
2 tablespoons clarified butter
1 cup veal or chicken stock
1/2 cup (1 stick) butter
Fresh chervil sprigs

Trim tenderloin and save trimmings for marinade. Prepare **Cranberry Marinade** and marinate meat for 12 hours. Remove meat and reserve marinade.

Preheat oven to 350 degrees. Season meat with salt and pepper, then sear in a hot sauté pan with clarified butter. Transfer tenderloin to a roasting pan and roast to desired doneness according to meat thermometer (about an hour for rare). Once meat has cooked, remove from pan, drain off fat, and deglaze pan with reserved **Cranberry Marinade**. Reduce combined marinade and pan drippings until mixture becomes syrupy. Add veal stock and reduce again to desired thickness. Finish by whisking in butter. Adjust seasonings. Serve meat topped with sauce and sprigs of fresh chervil.

For an appealing presentation, place meat in the center of a ring of caramelized small whole potatoes and tiny onions.

Serves 4

Cranberry Marinade

Meat trimmings from
  tenderloin
2 tablespoons vegetable oil
1 carrot, finely chopped
1 stalk celery, finely chopped
1/2 onion, finely chopped
1 teaspoon dried thyme
5 whole cloves
2 bay leaves
3 sprigs fresh parsley
1 (750-ml.) bottle Mouton
  Cadet wine
1 cup fresh cranberries

Sear meat trimmings in oil, then add carrot, celery, onion, thyme, cloves, bay leaves, and parsley. When both meat and vegetables are browned, deglaze pan with wine and simmer for 30 minutes. Strain and reserve liquid, discarding meat trimmings and herbs. Add cranberries and cool.

Makes about 2 cups

MARIUS
Le Meridien Hotel
2000 Second Avenue
Coronado, California 92118
(619) 435-3000

🦐 Sausage and Shrimp Cristo

2 links mild Italian sausage, casings removed and sliced diagonally in large ovals
8 jumbo shrimp, peeled and deveined, cut in half lengthwise
1/2 clove garlic, minced
1 green bell pepper, sliced
1/2 cup extra-virgin olive oil
1/2 cup dry white wine
1/2 cup besciamella sauce (see recipe on p. 28)
8 ounces fettuccine, cooked al dente
1/4 cup chopped fresh parsley
1/4 cup freshly grated Parmesan cheese

Sauté sausage, shrimp, garlic, and bell pepper in oil. Stir in white wine and besciamella sauce.

To serve, toss sausage and shrimp sauce with pasta. Garnish with chopped parsley and Parmesan cheese.

Serves 4

This is a family recipe developed by Uncle James Cristo over 45 years ago.

VALENTINO'S
11828 Rancho Bernardo Road
San Diego, California 92128
(619) 451-3200

Pork Scaloppine with Marsala Pesto Sauce, Artichokes, and Sun-Dried Tomatoes

12 (2-ounce) pork tenderloin
  medallions, pounded thin
6 tablespoons all-purpose flour
Salt and pepper to taste
1/4 cup vegetable oil
6 whole sun-dried tomatoes,
  julienned
2 large artichoke hearts, sliced
2 teaspoons pesto
1/2 cup Marsala wine
2 cups heavy cream

Coat pieces of pork with flour seasoned with salt and pepper. Heat oil in sauté pan and sauté medallions until brown on both sides. Remove pork from pan and set aside.

To same pan, add sun-dried tomatoes, artichoke slices, and pesto. Deglaze pan with Marsala wine. Add heavy cream and reduce mixture to consistency of light cream sauce. Return pork to pan while sauce is reducing. Adjust seasonings to taste. To serve, arrange medallions on dinner plates and ladle sauce over the top.

Serves 4

Chef Rick Huffman likes to serve this delicious dish on a bed of sauteéd bow-tie pasta, julienned bell peppers, and asparagus, topped with freshly grated Parmesan.

CROWN ROOM
Hotel Del Coronado
1500 Orange Avenue
Coronado, California 92118
(619) 435-6611

Sweet Endings

❈ Heavenly Chocolate Mousse

1 pound dark chocolate
7 eggs
2 cups heavy cream
1/2 cup brandy
8 large fresh strawberries

Melt chocolate in the top of a double boiler. Separate eggs and add slightly beaten egg yolks to the warm melted chocolate. Whip egg whites and fold into chocolate mixture. Next whip heavy cream and fold into chocolate mixture along with brandy. Chill until set, preferably overnight.

To serve, transfer mousse to champagne glasses using an ice cream scoop. Garnish each serving with a perfect fresh strawberry.

For an extra rich dessert, serve with a glass of Cabernet Sauvignon.

Serves 8

CAFE ELEVEN
1440 University Avenue
San Diego, California 92103
(619) 260-8023

❀ Chocolate Mousse Duet with Three Fresh Fruit Sauces

3 gelatin sheets or 3 envelopes
  unflavored gelatin
3-1/2 cups water
6 (1-ounce) squares dark
  chocolate
2 eggs
1 tablespoon rum
1-1/2 cups heavy cream (cold)
6 (1-ounce) squares white
  chocolate
1 tablespoon Grand Marnier
  liqueur
Dark chocolate shavings
White chocolate shavings
Mint leaves
Powdered sugar

To prepare dark chocolate mousse, let 1 gelatin sheet or envelope of gelatin soften in 1-3/4 cups water for a few minutes. Cut dark chocolate squares into small pieces and melt in a double boiler. Whisk 1 egg and rum together in a small bowl over hot water until warm. Add softened gelatin to egg mixture and let dissolve. Add melted dark chocolate, mix well, and cool to room temperature. Whip 3/4 cup cold cream and fold into dark chocolate mixture. Transfer mixture to a clean bowl and refrigerate for 1 hour.

To prepare white chocolate mousse, let 2 gelatin sheets or envelopes of gelatin soften in 1-3/4 cups water for a few minutes. Cut white chocolate squares into small pieces and melt in a double boiler. Whisk 1 egg and Grand Marnier together in a small bowl over hot water until warm. Add softened gelatin to egg mixture and let dissolve. Add melted white chocolate, mix well, and cool to room temperature. Whip 3/4 cup cold cream and fold into white chocolate mixture. Transfer mixture to a clean bowl and refrigerate for 1 hour.

To serve, pool a portion of each of **Three Fresh Fruit Sauces** on 4 cold dessert plates. Using an ice cream scoop, arrange dark and white mousses on top of sauces. Decorate dark mousse with white chocolate shavings and white mousse with dark chocolate shavings. Place mint leaves between mousses and sprinkle with powdered sugar.

Serves 4 generously

Three Fresh Fruit Sauces

1 cup sugar
1 cup water
2 ripe kiwis
2 cups red raspberries
1 ripe mango

Prepare a simple sugar syrup by boiling sugar and water together for about 5 minutes, then cool. Peel kiwis, cut into small pieces, puree in a food processor, and sweeten to taste with sugar syrup. Strain raspberries in a sieve to remove seeds, then add sugar syrup to taste. Peel mango, remove seed, and puree in food processor. Sweeten to taste with sugar syrup. Refrigerate sauces for 30 minutes before serving.

Makes 1 cup of each sauce

MILLE FLEURS
6009 Paseo Delicias
Rancho Santa Fe, California 92067
(619) 756-3085

❁ Licorice Mousse with Chocolate Sauce

1/2 cup sugar
1/4 cup water
About 2 teaspoons licorice
    powder (available at Boney's
    Markets throughout San
    Diego County or nationally
    at gourmet and specialty
    stores)
5 egg yolks
1-3/4 cups heavy cream

In a saucepan, stir together sugar, water, and licorice powder. (*Note:* Use amount of licorice powder specified as a guideline only; actual amount needed will vary with personal taste and freshness of powder.) Bring mixture to a boil to form a syrup, then remove from heat. Whip egg yolks in the top of a double boiler. Slowly whisk in licorice syrup, cooking until mixture thickens and forms "ribbons" when whisk is lifted from mixture. When thickened, transfer to a bowl and cool. Whip heavy cream and fold into licorice mixture. Place into molds and freeze overnight. Unmold and serve with warm **Chocolate Sauce**.

Serves 6 to 8

Chocolate Sauce

8 (1-ounce) squares sweet or
    semisweet chocolate
1 teaspoon heavy cream
3 tablespoons unsalted butter,
    softened

Melt chocolate in the top of a double boiler. Whisk in cream, followed by butter.

Makes about 3/4 cup

MARIUS
Le Meridien Hotel
2000 Second Avenue
Coronado, California 92118
(619) 435-3000

❀ Zabaglione

8 egg yolks
2 egg whites
1/2 cup sugar
1 cup Marsala wine
1/4 teaspoon ground cinnamon
1/2 teaspoon vanilla extract
Zest of 1 lemon or orange
Whipped cream
Ground nutmeg

Put egg yolks, egg whites, sugar, Marsala, cinnamon, and vanilla in the top of a double boiler. Cook over hot water, beating continuously until mixture thickens to a soft, pudding-like consistency. Add lemon or orange zest, mix, and pour into a dessert dish. Top with whipped cream, sprinkle with nutmeg, and serve. (*Note:* May also be served cold if preferred.)

Serves 4

DANTE'S
9379 Mira Mesa Boulevard
San Diego, California 92126
(619) 693-3252

❋ Gabriel's Magic Custard

4 cups milk
1 cup sugar
3 tablespoons butter or
    margarine
4 large eggs
2 tablespoons cornstarch

Place milk, sugar, and butter in a large saucepan and bring to a boil, stirring occasionally. Whisk eggs and cornstarch together and quickly whisk into hot milk mixture. Stir until mixture thickens (this will happen almost instantaneously). Remove from heat and pour into a shallow pan or four 8-ounce custard dishes. Cool, then refrigerate before serving.

As a variation, fold whipped cream and your choice of liqueur into the slightly cooled custard to create a Bavarian cream dessert. Or use the custard either to fill cream puffs or as an elegant filling between layers of cake. This basic recipe also lends itself well to flavorings such as chocolate, butterscotch, or banana—use 1 teaspoon of your favorite bottled extract.

Serves 4

GABY'S BAKERY AND DELI
113 East Grand Avenue
Escondido, California 92025
(619) 480-6801

❈ Burnt Cream

1-1/2 cups sugar
12 egg yolks
2 tablespoons vanilla extract
6 cups heavy cream
1 cup milk
6 teaspoons brown sugar

Preheat oven to 350 degrees. Combine sugar, egg yolks, and vanilla. Scald cream and milk together. Whisk a small amount of hot mixture into egg yolk mixture, then gradually add the rest. Pour combination into 6–8 large baking cups and place in a pan filled with enough water to reach halfway up the sides of the baking cups. Bake for 30 minutes or until custard is firm.

Before serving, sprinkle a teaspoon of brown sugar on the surface of each custard and place under broiler until sugar caramelizes.

Serves 6 to 8

PACIFICA DEL MAR
Del Mar Plaza
1555 Camino Del Mar
Del Mar, California 92014
(619) 792-0476

❊ Soufflé Glacé Parfait Amour in Chocolate Cups

6 egg yolks or equivalent egg
  substitute
3 egg whites
8 tablespoons sugar
3 cups whipped cream
1/4 cup Marie Brizard Parfait
  Amour liqueur, or substitute
  Blue Curaçao
6 cups raspberries
2 tablespoons Chambord
  liqueur
Fresh mint sprigs

Beat egg yolks with 2 tablespoons sugar until mixture becomes pale yellow. Whip egg whites with remaining 6 tablespoons sugar to form a smooth meringue. Using a spatula, fold yolk mixture into meringue, then slowly add Parfait Amour. Finish by folding in whipped cream. Distribute mixture among 8 **Chocolate Cups**, filling each to the top. Freeze for 3 hours.

Blend 4 cups raspberries with Chambord and strain to eliminate seeds. Pour a ring of raspberry sauce around the center of each dessert plate, then set a filled **Chocolate Cup** in the center of each. Garnish with remaining raspberries and mint sprigs.

Serves 8

Chocolate Cups

2 cups semisweet chocolate
  chips

Melt chocolate chips in the top of a double boiler. Smooth melted chocolate over the bottom and sides of 8 fluted cupcake papers. Put filled papers into custard cups for support and chill until very firm. When ready to fill, carefully peel off paper, taking care not to leave fingerprints on chocolate. Chill again before using. (*Note:* Some chefs use gloves to keep warm fingers from marking the chocolate.)

Makes 8

U.S. GRANT HOTEL
326 Broadway
San Diego, California 92101
(619) 232-3121

❈ Chocolate Pecan Pie

1-1/4 cups dark corn syrup
1 cup sugar
4 eggs
1 tablespoon vanilla extract
1 (1-ounce) square
   unsweetened chocolate
1 (1-ounce) square semisweet
   chocolate
1/2 cup (1 stick) butter
1 cup pecans
1 (9-inch) unbaked pie shell

Preheat oven to 350 degrees. Mix together corn syrup, sugar, eggs, and vanilla, taking care not to overbeat. Heat chocolates and butter until melted, then combine with sugar and egg mixture. Pour combination into unbaked pie shell and sprinkle with pecans. Bake for 60 to 75 minutes, or until firm. (*Note:* Cover with aluminum foil if nuts and/or crust start becoming too brown.)

Serves 8

SQUARE ONE
119 North Main Street
Fallbrook, California 92028
(619) 728-5154

❀ Mud Pie

1-1/2 cups Oreo cookie crumbs
4 tablespoons margarine,
    melted
1/2 cup caramel ice cream
    topping
1/2 gallon Dryer's Mud Pie ice
    cream, softened
1-1/2 cups chocolate sauce
Whipped cream
Maraschino cherries

Mix cookie crumbs with melted margarine and press into the bottom of a 9-inch springform pan. Swirl caramel topping over crust. Add ice cream and pack down firmly. Freeze until firm.

Remove from freezer, pour chocolate sauce evenly over pie, and shake until settled. Place back in freezer until ready to serve, then top with whipped cream and maraschino cherries.

Serves 8

BIG STONE LODGE
12237 Old Pomerado Road
Poway, California 92064
(619) 748-1135

✹ Mile-High Strawberry Pie

1/4 pound (1/2 stick) butter or
   margarine, melted
1/4 cup firmly packed brown
   sugar
1 cup all-purpose flour
1 (16-ounce) package frozen,
   sweetened strawberries
1/2 cup sugar
1 tablespoon fresh lemon juice
1/8 teaspoon salt
4 egg whites
1 cup heavy cream
1/4 cup powdered sugar
1 teaspoon vanilla extract

Combine first 3 ingredients and bake mixture in a pie pan at 375 degrees for about 15 minutes. Crumble pastry and cover the bottom of a 9-inch springform pan with crumbs, reserving some to use as a topping.

Mix strawberries, sugar, lemon juice, salt, and egg whites. Using an electric mixer, beat for 20 minutes, starting at low speed and gradually increasing to high. In a separate bowl, whip cream, powdered sugar, and vanilla. (Do not overwhip; peaks should be very soft.) Fold cream mixture into strawberry mixture. Pour strawberry filling onto crumb crust and sprinkle with reserved crumbs. Cover with plastic wrap and freeze overnight. (*Note:* May be prepared up to a week in advance.)

Try topping this silky creation with a thin raspberry puree.

Serves 10

SQUARE ONE
119 North Main Street
Fallbrook, California 92028
(619) 728-5154

✽ Bev's Best Apple Dumplings

4 large baking apples, cored
   (peeled if desired)
1 cup raisins
1/2 cup walnuts, coarsely
   chopped
2 tablespoons butter
1/2 teaspoon ground cinnamon
1/4 cup firmly packed brown
   sugar
6–7 tablespoons water
2 cups all-purpose flour
1/2 teaspoon salt
2/3 cup shortening
Cream or ice cream

Preheat oven to 350 degrees. Prepare filling by putting raisins, nuts, butter, cinnamon, brown sugar, and 1 tablespoon water into a saucepan. Heat until sugar dissolves, about 3 minutes, and then set aside.

To prepare dough, cut shortening into flour and salt. Stir in 5 to 6 tablespoons water until dough begins to round up into a ball. Press together, wrap in plastic, and let rest for 30 minutes before rolling out. (*Note:* Use frozen dough or a mix if time is short.)

Roll dough into a large square, then cut into quarters. Place an apple on top of each piece of dough, fill hollow cores with raisin-nut filling,and pull sides of dough around each apple. Press together at top, making folds while pinching it up around the filled apple. Place dumplings on a large flat baking dish and bake for 35 to 45 minutes. Spoon any remaining filling around the dumplings and serve with cream or ice cream.

Serves 4

BEV'S KOZY KITCHEN
138 West Grand Avenue
Escondido, California 92027
(619) 745-9265

✣ Glazed Banana Tart

1/3 cup blanched almonds
1-1/2 cups all-purpose flour
3/4 cup (1-1/2 sticks) plus 2
  tablespoons butter, cut into
  small pieces
1/4 cup plus 2 tablespoons
  powdered sugar
1 egg, beaten
2 tablespoons sugar
6 tablespoons heavy cream
8 (1-ounce) squares sweet
  chocolate, cut into small
  pieces
2 tablespoons rum
4–5 bananas, thinly sliced
3 tablespoons apricot preserves

Put almonds in a blender or food processor and pulverize to a powder. Whip flour, 3/4 cup butter, almond powder, and 1/4 cup powdered sugar together. Add half the beaten egg and mix to a dough consistency. Refrigerate for 1 hour.

Preheat oven to 350 degrees. Roll out dough to fit an 8-inch tart mold. Combine remaining half of beaten egg, 2 tablespoons sugar, 2 tablespoons butter, and 2 tablespoons powdered sugar, and pour mixture on top of molded dough. Bake for about 20 minutes, then remove from oven and cool to room temperature.

Bring cream to a boil. Reduce heat and carefully add chocolate, stirring until chocolate is melted. Add rum, then cool to room temperature.

When both cream-filled shell and chocolate sauce are cool, spread chocolate over the top of cream filling. Heat apricot preserves until melted, then put through a sieve to make a clear glaze. Arrange banana slices on top of chocolate layer. Dilute apricot glaze with a little water, if needed, and brush it over the surface of the bananas. Slice and serve.

Serves 6 to 8

L'ESCALE
Le Meridien Hotel
2000 Second Street
Coronado, California 92118
(619) 435-3000

✵ Grand Avenue Carrot Cake with Coconut Icing

1-1/2 cup vegetable oil
1-3/4 cups sugar
3 eggs
2 cups all-purpose flour
1 teaspoon baking powder
1 teaspoon baking soda
1/4 teaspoon salt
2 teaspoons ground cinnamon
2 cups peeled and grated
    carrots

Preheat oven to 375 degrees. Mix oil, sugar, and eggs until blended. Sift flour, baking powder, baking soda, salt, and cinnamon together. Add to moist ingredients and beat well. Stir in grated carrots. Pour batter into a well-greased and floured 10-inch Bundt pan. Bake for 50 minutes or until cake tests done. Cool, then frost with **Coconut Icing**.

Serves 12 to 16

Coconut Icing

1/2 cup shredded or pulverized
    sweetened coconut
2 cups powdered sugar
1/2 cup (1 stick) butter or
    margarine, softened

Put coconut into a food processor and pulse on and off to make finer pieces. Combine well with powdered sugar and butter. (*Note:* Bundt cakes look nice with icing drizzled over the top and down the sides. For this effect, thin frosting with milk or cream.)

Makes about 3 cups

GABY'S BAKERY AND DELI
113 East Grand Avenue
Escondido, California 92025
(619) 480-6801

❁ Apple Crisp

3 pounds apples, peeled,
   cored, and sliced
2-1/2 cups all-purpose flour
2-1/4 cups sugar
2 cups shredded cheddar
   cheese
1 cup (2 sticks) unsalted butter,
   melted
1 tablespoon ground cinnamon

Preheat oven to 325 degrees. Parboil and drain apple slices, and set aside.

Mix flour, 1-1/2 cups sugar, shredded cheese, and melted butter. (Mixture will be slightly lumpy.) Set aside.

In a large mixing bowl, mix apple slices, cinnamon, and remaining 3/4 cup sugar. Pour apple mixture into a large baking dish and top evenly with reserved crust mixture. Bake for 45 minutes or until golden brown. Serve in large glass goblets.

Top this hearty dessert with vanilla ice cream for an extra tasty treat.

Serves 6

GENTLEMAN'S CHOICE
1020 San Marcos Boulevard
San Marcos, California 92069
(619) 744-5215

❋ Molasses-Honey-Fruit Bars

2 cups sugar
1 cup (2 sticks) butter or
    margarine, softened
2 large eggs, slightly beaten
1 cup honey
1/2 cup molasses
Approximately 4-1/2 cups all-
    purpose flour
1 teaspoon baking soda
1 (15-ounce) box raisins
1/2 cup chopped nuts
    (optional)
1 cup candied fruit (optional)

Preheat oven to 375 degrees. Combine sugar, butter, and eggs, then stir in honey and molasses. Mix flour and baking soda together by sifting or stirring well. Add flour mixture to honey mixture and stir. Mix in raisins, nuts, and candied fruit. (*Note:* Dough should be stiff enough to roll out. If too sticky, add enough extra flour to bring it to this point; if too dry, add another egg or a few spoonfuls of milk.) Divide dough in half. Put each portion on a greased 12-by-15-inch jelly roll pan. Roll dough directly on baking sheet so that it becomes a large rectangle covering entire surface of sheet. Bake for about 12 minutes, then cool slightly and cut into 2-by-3-inch bars.

A couple of these and you should be strong enough to move a small piano.

Makes 5 dozen

GABY'S BAKERY AND DELI
113 East Grand Avenue
Escondido, California 92025
(619) 480-6801

❈ Hazelnut Cookies

3-1/4 cups all-purpose flour
1 (1-pound) box powdered
    sugar
4 eggs plus 3 egg yolks, beaten
1 teaspoon baking soda
2 tablespoons honey
1 pound whole hazelnuts,
    toasted and skins rubbed off

Preheat oven to 350 degrees. Combine flour, powdered sugar, whole eggs, baking soda, honey, and hazelnuts. Form mixture into 4 rolls, 1-1/2 inches in diameter. Transfer rolls to a large baking sheet and brush each with beaten egg yolks. Bake for 20 minutes. (Cookies will look very dark, almost like chocolate.) Allow cookie rolls to cool completely, then slice.

Make 3 to 4 dozen

LUIGI'S CUCINA ITALIANA
766 North Midway Drive
Escondido, California 92027
(619) 745-2250

❈ Olde English Sherry Trifle

1 (16-ounce) pound cake
2 tablespoons Bird's Custard
    Powder
2 tablespoons sugar
2 cups milk
1/3 cup raspberry jam
1 cup sherry or fruit juice
2 cups mixed fruit chunks (if
    using canned, drain well)
1 cup heavy cream, whipped
Sliced almonds
Maraschino cherries
Chocolate shavings

In a saucepan, combine custard powder with sugar. Add a small amount of milk to mixture, then stir in remainder. Cook over medium heat until mixture thickens. Cool completely.

Slice pound cake into 10 slices. Sandwich cake together with raspberry jam. Cut into strips and arrange around bottom and sides of a pretty glass dish so that jam filling makes vertical stripes. Sprinkle sherry or fruit juice over cake. (*Note:* If cake looks dry, use juice from the fruit to moisten.) Arrange fruit on top of cake, then cover with a layer of cooled custard. Pipe whipped cream on top of trifle and decorate with almonds, cherries, and chocolate shavings.

Serves 10

VINEYARD BAKERY
1115-1 East Valley Parkway
Escondido, California 92027
(619) 489-6458

Restaurants

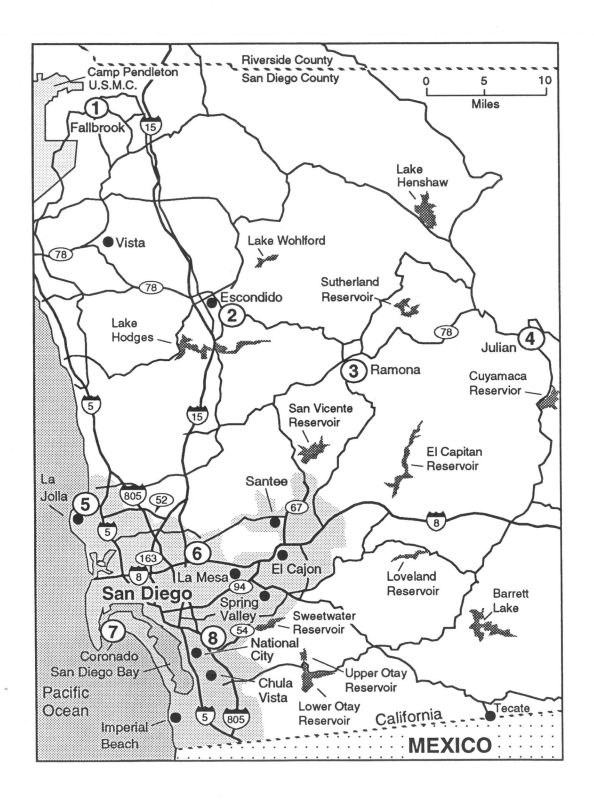

⚏ Restaurant Listings

The following listings offer additional information about the restaurants represented in the recipe sections of this book.

KEY:
Prices/credit cards: $ (under $10); $$ ($10 to $20); $$$ ($20 and up); ☐ (credit cards accepted); no ☐ (credit cards not accepted)
Dress: C (casual); D (dressy)
Map locations: (1) Fallbrook (2) North San Diego County (3) Ramona (4) East San Diego County (5) La Jolla-Del Mar (6) Old Town-USD Area (7) Coronado (8) Downtown-Balboa Park-National City

Anthony's Fish Grotto, 4120 La Jolla Village Dr., La Jolla, CA 92037; (619) 457-5008. The specialty here is seafood enhanced with creative sauces. Anthony's restaurants in many fine locations have been favored by San Diegans for decades. $$; ☐; C; (5)

Barcino Grill, Hyatt Regency La Jolla, 3777 La Jolla Village Dr., San Diego, CA 92122; (619) 552-1234. This casual spot offers something for everyone, with the specialty of "Cuisine Naturelle"— healthy, low-fat, low-calorie, yet flavorful foods. $$; ☐; C; (5)

Bev's Kozy Kitchen, 138 W. Grand Ave., Escondido, CA 92027; (619) 745-9265. Here's American-style home cooking in a bright cheerful kitchen. You'll feel like a "regular" on your first visit. The specialties are pot roast, Swiss steak, and apple dumplings. $; ☐; C; (2)

Big Stone Lodge, 12237 Old Pomerado Rd., Poway, CA 92064; (619) 748-1135. This is a historic lodge with authentic country atmosphere. The menu offers steaks, barbecued ribs and chicken, hamburgers, and chicken fried steak. Live music nightly. $$; ☐; C; (2).

Cafe Del Rey Moro, 1549 El Prado, Balboa Park, San Diego, CA 92101; (619) 234-8511. Within this historical landmark, designed after a Moorish palace in Spain, visitors find sunny garden terraces and antique-filled dining areas. Southwestern regional cuisine includes grilled fish with herbal butter, seafood, poultry, and beef. $ (lunch) and $$ (dinner); ☐; C; (8)

Cafe Eleven, 1440 University Ave., San Diego, CA 92103; (619) 260-8023. Here French country cuisine is served in a serene atmosphere of crisp white tablecloths and considerate service. Every dish is freshly prepared. Birthdays are often celebrated here. $$; ☐; C or D; (6)

Cafe Japengo, Hyatt Regency La Jolla, 3777 La Jolla Village Dr., San Diego, CA 92122; (619) 552-1234. Chosen by *San Diego Magazine's 1992 Annual Dining and Nightlife Guide* as both Best Sushi Bar and Best Japanese Restaurant, here Chef Moogk develops many enticing dishes. $$; □; C; (5)

Cajun Connection, 740 Nordahl Rd. #114, San Marcos, CA 92069; (619) 741-5680. Try Louisiana Cajun food cooked and served by the friendly Kerner family. Their jambalaya, blackened fish, oysters, catfish, and shrimp creole will take you to the bayou. $$; □; C; (2)

Carlos Murphy's, Corporate Office, 6680 Convoy Ct., San Diego, CA 92111; (619) 576-3840. The offerings here are coastal Mexican cuisine: fajitas, fish and shrimp tacos, barbecue, salads, and burgers. The decor is bright and snappy, and the service is friendly. $; □; C; check Yellow Pages for nearest location

Casa de Bandini, 2754 Calhoun St., San Diego, CA 92110; (619) 297-8211. This historic restaurant in the romantic Bazaar del Mundo surrounds diners in Old California elegance. Especial de la casa: top sirloin in soft tacos and carnitas. $; □; C; (6)

Casa de Pico, 2754 Calhoun St., San Diego, CA 92110; (619) 296-3276. Also located in the Bazaar del Mundo, this casual Mexican eatery serves birdbath-sized margaritas and delicious enchiladas. $; □; C; (6)

China Wharf, 1020 W. San Marcos Blvd., San Marcos, CA 92069; (619) 744-8888. A large glass window to the kitchen provides diners with a view of flames leaping around the woks. Exciting! Chinese and Thai dishes abound. $$; □; C; (2)

Crown Room, Hotel Del Coronado, 1500 Orange Ave., Coronado, CA 92118; (619) 435-6611. California cuisine arrives at the table here with a touch of French refinement in surroundings of world-class elegance. Specialties are steaks and seafood. $$ (lunch) and $$$ (dinner); □; D; (7)

Dansk Restaurant, 8425 La Mesa Blvd., La Mesa, CA 91941; (619) 463-0640. Continental with a predominantly Scandinavian flair. Swedish pancakes, Danish sausage, Swedish meatballs, Chicken Iceland, and more are served in a quaint atmosphere. $; □; C; (4)

Dante's, 9379 Mira Mesa Blvd., San Diego, CA 92126; (619) 693-3252. This quietly elegant place has been reviewed and named San Diego's "Most Romantic Restaurant." Lovely antiques, soft lighting, piano music, and continental cuisine add to the aura. $$; □; C or D; (2)

El Bizcocho, Rancho Bernardo Inn, 17550 Bernardo Oaks Dr., San Diego, CA 92128; (619) 487-1611. Elegant French cuisine is served here in an atmosphere of quiet refinement. A background pianist enhances the rich ambience and exquisite furnishings. $$$; ☐; D; (2)

El Tecolote, 6110 Friars Rd., San Diego, CA 92108; (619) 295-2087. "The Owl" wisely prepares traditional Mexican food. Try the Beef Tongue Vera Cruz, the Mole Poblano, or one of the great vegetarian dishes and see why this spot has garnered the San Diego Restaurant Critics Award and two Silver Fork Awards. $$; ☐; C; (6)

Filippi's Pizza Grotto, General Office, 9969 Mira Mesa Blvd., Suite 5, San Diego, CA 92131 (619) 695-1441. A long-time favorite of pizza lovers, here diners feast on many great pasta dishes as well. $; ☐; C; check Yellow Pages for nearest location

The Fireside, 439 W. Washington Ave., Escondido, CA 92025; (619) 745-1931. This fine steakhouse serves dry aged beef. The large stone fireplace and luxuriously thick padded booths lend a gracious atmosphere to dining. $$; ☐; C or D; (2)

Gaby's Bakery and Deli, 113 E. Grand Ave., Escondido, CA 92025; (619) 480-6801. You'll find Gaby's reminiscent of a Parisian sidewalk cafe, with murals on the walls and striped awnings over cases of delightful bakery items. Offerings include light lunches and lots of desserts. $; no ☐; C; (2)

Gentleman's Choice, 1020 San Marcos Blvd., San Marcos, CA 92069; (619) 744-5215. The menu here features award-winning prime rib and excellent seafood. Flavorful American-style cooking is served in a warm, cozy, country atmosphere. $$; ☐; C; (2)

Hamburguesa, 2754 Calhoun St., San Diego, CA 92110; (619) 295-0584. Amid Old California elegance, strolling mariachis enhance the atmosphere of historic Bazaar del Mundo. The Mexican cuisine here straddles gourmet hamburgers, salads, and desserts. $; ☐; C; (6)

Joe's Italian Dinners, 403 W. Grand Ave., Escondido, CA 92025; (619) 741-2935. This romantic Italian restaurant transports one to another time and another place. Joe's is quiet, cozy, and serene. Veal dishes are specialties of the house. $$; no ☐; C; (2)

Lawrence Welk Resort, 8840 Lawrence Welk Dr., Escondido, CA 92026; (619) 749-3253. American and Continental cuisine are served in a relaxing atmosphere at this famous resort. Naturally, there's a pleasant musical background. $$; ☐; C; (2)

L'Escale, Le Meridien Hotel, 2000 2nd Ave., Coronado, CA 92118 (619) 435-3000. Here both Continental and California cuisine are served with a French flair. The atmosphere is warm and relaxed, the specialty is seafood. Enjoy dining on a lovely outdoor terrace. $$; □; C; (7)

Lino's, 2754 Calhoun St., San Diego, CA 92110; (619) 299-7124. Also in historic Bazaar del Mundo, this Italian ristorante offers a casual yet romantic ambience. Pasta specialties mingle with pizza, sandwiches, salads, and desserts. $$; □; C; (6)

Longhorn Cafe, 6519 Mission Gorge Rd., San Diego, CA 92120; (619) 283-0831. This is a high-spirited, no-nonsense sports bar and grill, where locals watch wide screen TV and eat great burgers. Long-time San Diegans say, "You'll never get a bum steer at the Longhorn." $; □; C; (6)

Luigi's Cucina Italiana, 766 N. Midway Dr., Escondido, CA 92027; (619) 745-2250. Imagine a family dinner in a big happy Italian household. Luigi's is neat, clean, comfortable, and warm. The specialties are pasta dishes, veal, and fish. $$; □; C; (2)

Marius, Le Meridien Hotel, 2000 2nd Ave., Coronado, CA 92118 (619) 435-3000. Provençal French, the specialties here are lobster and lamb—the best of land and sea! Celebrate a special occasion in a most elegant and intimate atmosphere. $$$; □; D; (7)

McDini's, 105 E. 8th St., National City, CA 91950; (619) 474-6771. This is a sports bar and restaurant that's been specializing in great corned beef and cabbage since the spring of 1890. McDini's has been owned for over 100 years by the Dini family. $; □; C; (8)

Mille Fleurs, 6009 Paseo Delicias, Rancho Santa Fe, CA 92067; (619) 756-3085. Elegant haute cuisine comes to the table here in a most romantic setting. The menu changes daily to accommodate the freshest and finest ingredients available. $$$; □; D; (2)

Ocean Terrace, Hotel Del Coronado, 1500 Orange Ave., Coronado, CA 92118 (619) 435-6611. This is California bistro fare *al fresco*. Dine casually on sandwiches and salads at this often-photographed historic hotel. $$, □; C; (7)

Ocean Terrace Grille, Hotel Del Coronado, 1500 Orange Ave., Coronado, CA 92118; (619) 435-6611. Specializing in seafood, this restaurant serves appetizers and light dinner entrees prepared on an open broiler. Enjoy casual outdoor dining beside picturesque San Diego Bay. $$; □; C; (7)

Pacifica Del Mar, Del Mar Plaza, 1555 Camino Del Mar, Del Mar, CA 92014; (619) 792-0476. Seafood dishes here are seasoned with imagination and good taste, and desserts are decadent. Visitors are treated to whimsically elegant decor and friendly service. $$; □; C or D; (5)

Pine Valley House, Old Hwy. 80, Pine Valley, CA 91962 (619) 473-8708. This historic old inn in picturesque Pine Valley offers American food in cozy surroundings. The house specialty here is prime rib; try it by the huge stone fireplace on a winter evening. $$; □; C or D; (4)

Prince of Wales, Hotel Del Coronado, 1500 Orange Ave., Coronado, CA 92118; (619) 435-6611. This gourmet restaurant blends traditional and modern elegance. Truly fit for a prince, the specialties are Steak Diane, seafood, and the Caesar salad. $$$; □; D; (7)

Quail's Inn, 1035 La Bonita Dr., San Marcos, CA 92069; (619) 744-2445. Elegant dining here offers a spectacular view of Lake San Marcos along with fresh seafood, prime rib, and an outstanding salad bar. The cocktail hour features exceptional appetizers. $$; □; C; (2)

Ruperto's Mexican Food, 1010 W. El Norte Pkwy., Escondido, CA 92026; (619) 743-9720. This is wonderful food served in a clean but plain atmosphere. A no frills, no fuss Mexican eatery that features great carne asada tacos! Take out is available. $; no □; C; (2)

San Vicente Inn and Golf Club, 24157 San Vicente Rd., Ramona, CA 92065 (619) 789-8290. Diners here enjoy creative cuisine served in a garden setting. Take in the view of a beautiful golf course on one side and the grandeur of the mountains on the other. $$; □; C; (3)

Square One, 119 N. Main St., Fallbrook, CA 92028; (619) 728-5154. After a pleasant drive to a lovely sequestered community among the avocado groves of North County, feast on soups, sandwiches, salads, and a marvelous selection of desserts. $; □; C; (1)

Torrey Pines Inn, 11480 N. Torrey Pines Rd., La Jolla, CA 92037; (619) 453-4420. The fresh California-style food here mingles with a Southwestern accent. Casual elegance and excellent service accompany a view of the unique Torrey Pines. Weekend diners find a noteworthy Sunday brunch. $$; □; C; (5)

U.S. Grant Hotel, 326 Broadway, San Diego, CA 92101; (619) 232-3121. Continental cuisine is served here in a club-like atmosphere that's historic, intimate, elegant, warm, and comfortable. Spoil yourself on house specialties of fresh seafood, rack of lamb, and venison. $$; □; D; (8)

Valentino's, 11828 Rancho Bernardo Rd., San Diego, CA 92128; (619) 451-3200. The gourmet Northern Italian food here comes from old family recipes. Elegant yet comfortable surroundings offer treats such as flambéed desserts prepared tableside. Harp music three nights a week. $ (lunch) and $$ (dinner); ☐; C; (2)

Vineyard Bakery, 1511-1 E. Valley Pkwy., Escondido, CA 92027; (619) 489-6458. Morning guests here feast on fragrant coffee and muffins; afternoon arrivals refresh themselves with tea and English pastries. Enjoy the coziness inside or relax in the sun outside beside a splashing fountain. $; no ☐; C; (2)

ᛦ Restaurant Index

⅏ Recipe Index

The bold asterisk (*) preceding a recipe title indicates a "recipe within a recipe"; that is, one that appears within the preparation instructions for a primary recipe, but which in some cases could stand alone or be served with another favorite dish.

BEGINNINGS

Shrimp Filippi, 29
Sopa del Mar, 18
Sugar-Cured Salmon with Chinese Mustard, 30
    *Sugar/Spice Mix, 30
    *Chinese Mustard, 30
Warm Veal Sweetbread Salad with Honey-Mustard Dressing, 9
    *Honey-Mustard Dressing, 9
West Coast Vegetable Salad, 7

MAIN COURSES

Aldo's Fresh Trout Calamari, 65
Barbequed Salmon Wrapped in Foil, 54
Black Bean Chili, 41
Buffalo Tenderloin with Cranberries, 90
    *Cranberry Marinade, 91
Cajun Chicken Fricassee, 69
Camarones Calientes, 47
Caneton à la Normande au Poivre Vert with Golden Apple Slices, 78
    *Golden Apple Slices, 78
Caribbean Sea Bass with Papaya Salsa, 64
    *Papaya Salsa, 64
Carne Asada Tacos, 87
Chicken and Sausage Jambalaya, 70
Chicken Fajitas, 71
Chicken St. Tropez, 76
Corned Beef and Cabbage, 83
Del Coronado Shore Plate, 52
    *Garlic Butter, 52
Especial de la Casa de Bandini, 88
Fettuccine Matrigiana, 42
Frijoles Refritos, 40
Grilled Ahi with Orange-Pineapple Salsa, 60
    *Orange-Pineapple Salsa, 60
Grilled Shrimp Tacos with Tomatillo Mayonnaise, 48
    *Carne Asada Marinade, 49
    *Tomatillo Mayonnaise, 49
Grilled Spring Lamb Chops with Garlic and Rosemary Butter Sauce, 79
    *Garlic and Rosemary Butter Sauce, 79
Grilled Swordfish on Wakame with Mango Lychee Relish and
    Lemongrass Essence, 58
        *Lemongrass Essence, 59
        *Mango Lychee Relish, 58
        *Wakame Seaweed, 59

SWEET ENDINGS

Vegetables

Potato - cheese fritters 20
Cauliflower - cheese fritters 21

Beginnings

Pine Valley Salad dressing 4
Cucumber - dill salad 5
Square one Veg Salad 7
Tortilla shell for salad 8
Honey mustard dressing 9

Soup

Square one Gazpacho 14
   "   " Chicken cheese 15
Tortilla Soup 16 & 17
Black Bean Chili 41

🎴 About the Author

San Diego County is home to Gwenn Jensen. A native, she earned her bachelor's and master of science degrees at San Diego State University, majoring in home economics with a specialty in foods and nutrition. As a 20-year veteran of teaching home ec in San Diego County high schools, community colleges, and adult schools, she knows how to make recipes easy to follow for the at-home cook.

For the past five years she's been heard on "Gwenn's Kitchen Talk," a taped daily radio presentation aired on KELY radio in Ely, Nevada. She also publishes a monthly newsletter under the same name, *Gwenn's Kitchen Talk*, a vehicle for hints, recipes, nutritional advice,and food trivia. She is a past president of the National League of American Pen Women, La Jolla Chapter and is a member of the American Institute of Wine and Food, San Diego Chapter.

Gwenn and her husband, Mogens, make their home in the North County. When she is not peering over the shoulder of one of the San Diego chefs, gathering information, she probably is preparing samples for her family and friends. Or she may be out taking a tap or ballet lesson, reasoning that as long as one keeps dancing or involved in an equally vigorous activity, the longer cooking and eating may be enjoyed.

Seafood

Grilled Salmon with spices 30
Scallops parisienne 32
Grilled shrimp & fruit 34
* Shrimp - mustard on pasta 46
** Grilled Shrimp Tacos 48
* Mustard Crusted Salmon 53
Salmon + herbs in foil 54
Salmon - Shrimp sauce - 55
Grilled Fish - Pineapple Salsa 60
" " Papaya salsa 64
* Sausage + Shrimp Pasta 92

Poultry

* Grilled Chicken Kabobs 68
** Fried Chicken + onions 69
Cajun Jambalaya - 70
** Chicken fajitas 70
Chicken enchiladas
tomatillo sauce 73
xxx Macadamia Chicken 75
xxx Chicken breast sun
dried tomato 76
Kung Pao Chicken 77

Beef - Veal Pork

* Filet stuffed Blue cheese 86
** " " with Crab 89
** Pork Tenderloin sun
dried tomatos artichokes 93

Desserts

* Choc. Mousse 97
White + dark Choc mousse 98
** Burnt Cream - 103
Liquier soufflé in
Choc. Cups - 104
** Choc. Pecan pie 105
+ Mud Pie 106
xxx Square one strawberry
dessert 107
Baked apple - cheese crisp 111
Hazelnut cookies 113